Contents at a Glance

Table of Contents

About the Author

Paul McFedries is a Microsoft Office expert and full-time technical writer. Paul has been authoring computer books since 1991 and has more than 80 books to his credit, which combined have sold more than 4 million copies worldwide. His titles include the Que Publishing books *Formulas and Functions with Microsoft Excel 2013* and *Windows 8 In Depth* (with coauthor Brian Knittel), as well as the Sams Publishing book *Windows 7 Unleashed*. Paul is also the proprietor of Word Spy (www.wordspy.com), a website devoted to *lexipionage*, the sleuthing of new words and phrases that have entered the English language. Please drop by Paul's personal website at www.mcfedries. com or follow Paul on Twitter at twitter.com/paulmcf and twitter.com/ wordspy.

Dedication

To Karen

Acknowledgments

If you re-read your work, you can find on re-reading a great deal of repetition can be avoided by re-reading and editing.

—William Safire

In the fast-paced world of computer book writing, where deadlines come whooshing at you at alarming speeds and with dismaying regularity, rereading a manuscript is a luxury reserved only for those who have figured out how to live a 36-hour day. Fortunately, every computer book *does* get reread—not once, not twice, but *many* times. I speak, of course, not of the diligence of this book's author but of the yeoman work done by this book's many and various editors, those sharp-eyed, red-pencil-wielding worthies whose job it is to make a book's author look good. Near the front of the book you'll find a long list of those hard-working professionals. However, there are a few folks I worked with directly, and I'd like to single them out for extra credit. A big, heaping helping of thanks goes out to acquisitions editor Loretta Yates, development editor Todd Brakke, project editor Betsy Gratner, copy editor Karen Annett, and technical editor Laura Acklen. A heaping helping of thanks to you all!

We Want to Hear from You!

As the reader of this book, *you* are our most important critic and commentator. We value your opinion and want to know what we're doing right, what we could do better, what areas you'd like to see us publish in, and any other words of wisdom you're willing to pass our way.

We welcome your comments. You can email or write to let us know what you did or didn't like about this book—as well as what we can do to make our books better.

Please note that we cannot help you with technical problems related to the topic of this book.

When you write, please be sure to include this book's title and author as well as your name and email address. We will carefully review your comments and share them with the author and editors who worked on the book.

Email: feedback@quepublishing.com

Mail: Que Publishing
ATTN: Reader Feedback
800 East 96th Street
Indianapolis, IN 46240 USA

Reader Services

Visit our website and register this book at quepublishing.com/register for convenient access to any updates, downloads, or errata that might be available for this book.

Create a new document

Open an existing document

Save your work

Print a document

Close a document

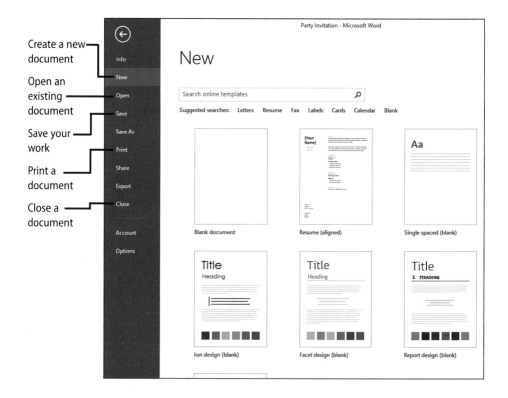

In this chapter, you'll learn about starting the Office RT programs, working with documents, and saving your work.

→ Starting the Office RT applications
→ Creating a new document
→ Preserving your work
→ Working with documents

Getting Started with Office RT

Most of this book deals with the specific features of the four Office RT applications—Word, Excel, PowerPoint, and OneNote—and a bit later you'll learn all of the most useful and practical techniques that these powerful programs have to offer. However, these programs also have quite a few features in common and some of these tools and techniques are the most useful and the most important. Sample techniques that fall into these categories are creating documents, saving documents, and printing documents.

This chapter takes you through all of these techniques. You'll also learn how to start and quit the Office RT applications, use templates, switch from one document to another, and more.

Starting the Office RT Applications

Whether you have a memo to write, a budget to build, a presentation to create, or some notes to jot down, the Office RT applications have the tools to help you get the job done. To get those tools onscreen, you need to start the application you want to use.

Starting an Office RT Application from the Start Screen

The easiest way to start any Office RT application is via the Windows RT Start screen.

1. In the Start screen, scroll right.

___

Scrolling the Start Screen

If you have a touchscreen, use your finger or a digital stylus to swipe the screen from right to left. If you have a mouse, either turn the scroll wheel or jiggle the mouse slightly to display the scroll bar at the bottom of the screen and then drag the scroll box to the right.

___

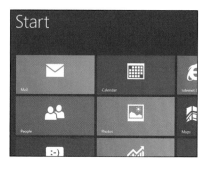

2. Select the tile for the Office RT application you want to use.

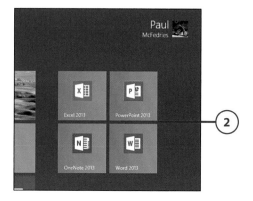

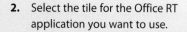

PINNING AN OFFICE RT APPLICATION TO THE START SCREEN

If you don't see the Office RT applications on your Windows RT Start screen, you need to pin them there yourself. Display the Start screen and then begin typing the name of the application you want to pin. When you see a tile for the application appear in the Apps search results, swipe down on (or right-click) the tile and then select Pin to Start. Windows RT adds a tile for the application to the Start screen.

Starting an Office RT Application from the Desktop

If you are currently working in the Windows RT desktop, you can also start any Office RT application via the taskbar.

1. To display the taskbar on a touchscreen, use your finger or a digital stylus to swipe down on the bottom edge of the desktop. If you have a mouse, move the mouse pointer to the bottom of the screen to reveal the taskbar.

2. Select the taskbar button for the Office RT application you want to use.

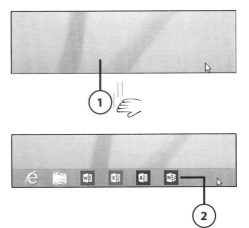

PINNING AN OFFICE RT APPLICATION TO THE TASKBAR

If you don't see the Office RT applications on the taskbar, you can pin them there yourself. Use the method in the previous section to start the Office RT application you want to pin. Tap and hold (or right-click) the running application's taskbar button and then select Pin This Program to Taskbar. Windows RT leaves a button for the application on the taskbar even after you quit the application.

Quitting an Office RT Application

When you've completed your work in an Office RT application, you should quit the program. This reduces clutter on the desktop and saves system resources to allow your other running program to operate more quickly. When you quit an Office RT application, be sure to save any documents that have unsaved changes so you do not lose your work.

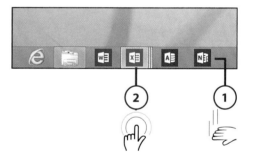

1. Use your finger or a digital stylus to swipe down on the bottom edge of the desktop (or move the mouse pointer to the bottom of the screen) to reveal the taskbar.

2. Tap and hold (or right-click) the taskbar icon of the Office RT application you want to quit.

3. Select Close All Windows. If the application has only one document open, select Close Window, instead.

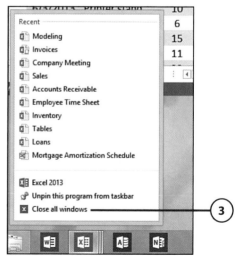

4. If the application prompts you to save changes before closing a document, select Save.

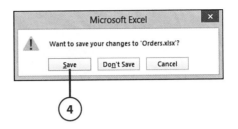

Quickly Closing an Application

If you have a mouse (or trackpad) and keyboard connected to your Windows RT device, an easier way to quit an Office RT application is to hold down the Shift key and click the Close (X) icon in the upper-right corner of any of the application's open windows.

Adding the Exit Command

The Office RT applications lack an Exit command that quits the application. However, such a command does exist and you can gain access to it by adding it to the Quick Access Toolbar. See the section "Customizing the Quick Access Toolbar" in Chapter 15, "Customizing the Office RT Applications."

Creating a New Document

To perform work in an Office RT application, you must first either create a new document or open an existing document. In this section, you learn about creating new documents.

Although OneNote creates a notebook for you to use as soon as you start the application, the other Office RT applications—Word, Excel, and PowerPoint—don't create a new document for you automatically. Instead, if you don't need to open an existing document, then you must create a new document by hand when you launch these applications. In each case, you can either create a blank document that is devoid of data and formatting, or you can create a document from a template, which is a special file that includes prefabricated content and formatting.

SAVING TIME WITH TEMPLATES

One secret to success in the business world is to let the experts do whatever it is they are good at. Let the salespeople sell, the copywriters write, and the designers design. If you try to do these things yourself, chances are that it will take you longer and the results will not be as good.

You can apply the same idea to the Office world, as well. Why spend endless hours tweaking the design and layout of, say, a brochure when a wide variety of professionally designed brochures is just a few screen taps away? I am talking here about using *templates*, special documents that come with predefined layouts, color schemes, graphics, and text.

Creating a Blank Document at Startup

You can create a new, blank document as soon as you start Word, Excel, or PowerPoint.

1. Start the application you want to use.

2. Select the blank option, such as Word's Blank Document icon.

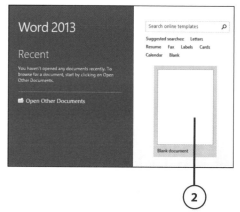

Creating a Blank Document After an Office RT Application Is Running

If you are already using Word, Excel, or PowerPoint, you can create a new, blank document from within the application.

1. Select File.

2. Select New to display the New tab.

Keyboard Shortcut

You can also display the New tab by pressing Ctrl+N.

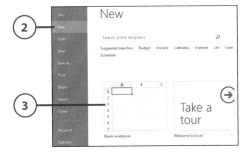

3. Select the blank option, such as Excel's Blank Workbook icon.

Creating a Document from a Template

Microsoft Office Online has well over 1,000 templates that you can use, divided into more than 20 different categories such as Brochures, Business Cards, Flyers, Letters and Letterhead, Memos and Fax Covers, and Newsletters. And that's just for Word. Hundreds of other templates are also available for Excel and PowerPoint. All of them were created by professional designers and most are quite striking. Of course, once you have created a document based on one of these templates, you're free to tweak the layout, design, and text to suit your needs.

1. Select File.

2. Select New to display the New tab.

Keyboard Shortcut

You can also display the New tab by pressing Ctrl+N.

3. If you see the template you want to use, select it and skip to step 8.

4. Use the search box to type a word or phrase that describes the type of template you want to use.

5. Select Search.

6. Select a category.

7. Select the template you want to use.

8. Select Create to download the template and create the new document based on the template.

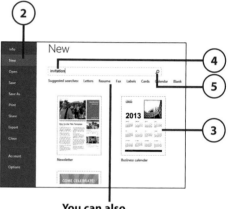

You can also select any of these sample searches.

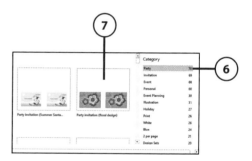

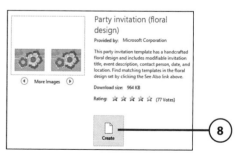

Preserving Your Work

Losing precious data due to a system crash is a constant, nagging worry for PC users. Why is it such a problem? The main reason is that when you work with a document, your PC takes a copy of the document from the hard drive and loads that copy into memory. This makes it much faster to work with the file, but the downside is that all the data loaded into memory is lost when your PC crashes or loses power. This means that if you've made changes to your document, those changes are lost when the memory is wiped.

To prevent this calamity, you need to save your document at regular intervals. Saving the document writes your changes to the hard drive file. Because your hard drive doesn't lose its data when your PC crashes or there's a power outage, your changes are safe and sound. To minimize the amount of work lost if your document shuts down without warning (and therefore minimize the amount of time you have to spend redoing that work), get into the habit of saving frequently, at least every few minutes. Some people save every time they pause in their work.

Saving a New Document

Although saving an existing document is a simple matter of selecting File, Save (or selecting the Save button in the Quick Access Toolbar or pressing Ctrl+S), saving a new document takes a few more steps.

1. Select File.
2. Select Save As to display the Save As tab.

Keyboard Shortcut
You can also display the Save As tab for a new document by pressing Ctrl+S.

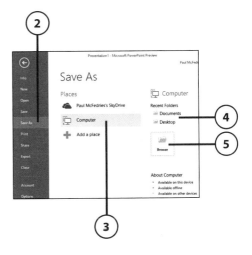

3. Select Computer.
4. If you see the folder you want to use to store the document, select it and skip to step 7.
5. Select Browse to open the Save As dialog box.

6. Select a folder that you want to use to store the document.

7. Type a name for the document.

8. Select Save.

File Naming Guidelines

The complete pathname for any document must not exceed 255 characters. The pathname includes not only the filename, but also the location of the document, including the drive letter, colon, folder name (or names), and backslashes. The filename can include any alphanumeric character, one or more spaces, and any of the following characters:

~ ` @ # $ % ^ & ( ) _ - + = { } [ ] ; , . '

The filename must not include any of the following characters:

* | \ : " < > ?

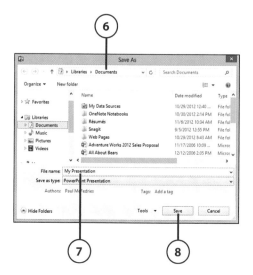

Go Further >>>

AUTORECOVER: SHORT, BUT NOT *TOO* SHORT

The Office RT applications come with a feature called AutoRecover that automatically saves your changes as you work. If your PC should crash before you get a chance to save, AutoRecover can usually recover most of your unsaved changes. If AutoRecover has a downside, it's that the default interval for saving the recovery data is every 10 minutes. That might sound quite short, but when you're on a roll you can get quite a bit of work done in 10 minutes. To help AutoRecover reclaim even more of your work, you can shorten the interval. Select File, Options, select the Save tab, use the Save AutoRecover Information Every *X* Minutes text box to reduce the number of minutes to the value you want to use, and then select OK.

For small documents, the shorter the AutoRecover interval, the better. If you regularly deal with only small documents, go ahead and drop the AutoRecover interval down to a minute. However, for large documents, saving the AutoRecover data can take the program a noticeable amount of time, so a very short interval can slow you down. Try a 4- or 5-minute interval as a compromise.

Saving a Document as a Copy

When you work in Microsoft Office, one of the best ways to save time and increase your efficiency is to, as the saying goes, avoid reinventing the wheel. This means, in this case, that if you need to create a document that is very similar to an existing document, don't build the new document from scratch. Instead, use the existing document as a starting point and modify it as needed for the new file.

1. Select File.

2. Select Save As to display the Save As tab.

3. Select Computer.

4. If you see the folder you want to use to store the document, select it and skip to step 7.

5. Select Browse to open the Save As dialog box.

6. Select a folder that you want to use to store the document.

7. Type a name for the document.

File Naming Guidelines

To avoid overwriting the existing document, make sure you select a different folder, specify a different filename, or both.

8. Select Save.

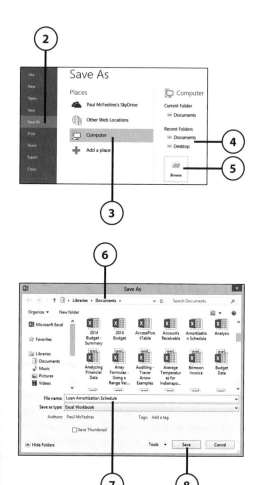

Saving a Document as a Different File Type

Word, Excel, and PowerPoint each have a default type of file that they create automatically when you save a new document. These default file types are named, respectively, Word Document, Excel Workbook, and PowerPoint Presentation. However, these applications also support a number of other file types. For example, if you want to share a Word file with someone who uses an older version of Office, you can save the file using the Word 97–2003 Document file type.

1. Select File.

2. Select Save As to display the Save As tab.

3. Select Computer.

4. If you see the folder you want to use to store the document, select it and skip to step 7.

5. Select Browse to open the Save As dialog box.

6. Select a folder that you want to use to store the document.

7. Type a name for the document.

8. Use the Save as Type list to select the file type you want to use.

9. Select Save.

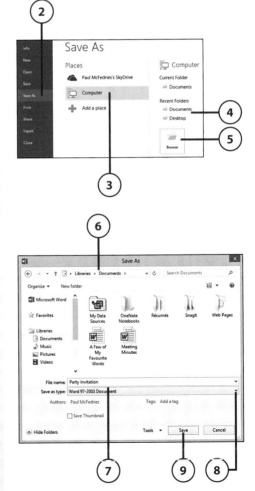

Working with Documents

You'll spend almost all of your Office RT time writing, editing, and formatting documents, but you'll also regularly face more mundane document chores, such as opening documents, switching from one open document to another, printing documents, and closing those documents you no longer need. The rest of this chapter takes you through these day-to-day document tasks.

Opening a Document

When you launch an Office RT application, the program first displays a window that includes a Recent list, which shows the last few documents that you've worked with in the application. You can reopen a document by selecting it from that list. If you don't see the document you want, then you need to use the Open dialog box to select the file.

1. Select File.

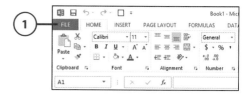

Opening a Document at Startup

If you're just starting the application and you don't see the document you want in the Recent list, select Open Other *Type*, where *Type* depends on the application: Document for Word, Workbook for Excel, or Presentation for PowerPoint.

2. Select Open to display the Open tab.

Keyboard Shortcut

You can also display the Open tab by pressing Ctrl+O.

3. Select Computer.

4. If you see the folder where the document is stored, select it and skip to step 7.

5. Select Browse to display the Open dialog box.

6. Select the folder that contains the document you want to open.

7. Select the document.

8. Select Open.

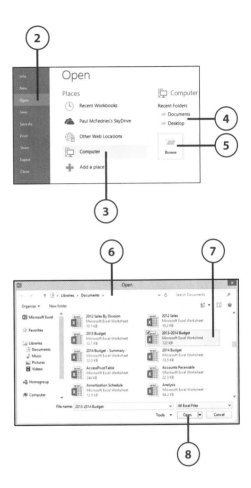

Switching Between Documents

If you have two or more documents open in an Office RT application, you can often switch from one document to another by tapping the other document's window. If you can't see the other document, then you must use the taskbar to switch to the other document.

1. Use your finger or a digital stylus to swipe down on the bottom edge of the desktop to reveal the taskbar. (If you have a mouse, move the pointer to the bottom of the screen.)

2. Select the taskbar button for the Office RT application you are using.

3. Select the document you want to use.

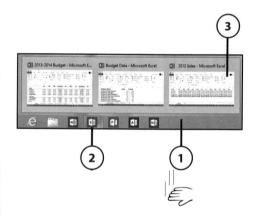

Keyboard Shortcut

You can also switch to a different document by holding down the Alt key and then tapping Tab until the icon for the document you want is selected, then release Alt.

Printing a Document

If you have a printer connected to your PC and you require a hard copy of the document you're working on, you can send the document to your printer.

1. Select File.

2. Select Print to display the Print tab.

Keyboard Shortcut

You can also display the Print tab by pressing Ctrl+P.

3. Select these arrows to preview the pages in the document.

4. If you have more than one printer, use this list to select the one you want to use to print the document.

5. Specify the number of copies you want to print.

6. Select Print.

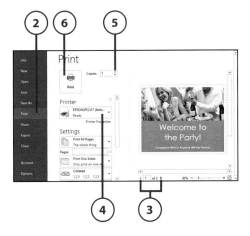

>>>Go Further

SPECIFYING PRINT SETTINGS

The Settings section of the Print tab offers a number of useful options that enable you to control your print jobs. The options vary between the Office RT applications, but in all the programs you can choose how much of the document you want to print (for example, every page or just selected pages), one-sided or two-sided printing, whether multiple-copy print jobs are collated (the entire document is printed before moving on to the next copy) or uncollated (all the page 1s are printed, then all the page 2s, and so on), the print orientation (portrait or landscape), the paper size, and the margin sizes.

Closing a Document

When you have completed your work on a document, you should close it to reduce clutter on the desktop and make it easier to switch between the other open documents.

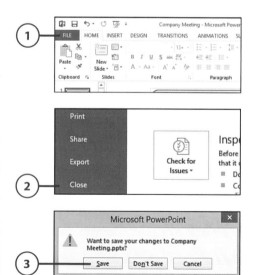

1. Select File.

2. Select Close. If you have unsaved changes, the application prompts you to save the file.

Keyboard Shortcut

You can also select the Close command by pressing Ctrl+F4.

3. Select Save to preserve your work and close the document.

Closing Shortcut

You can also close a document by selecting the Close icon (X) that appears in the upper-right corner of the document window.

Set the text
font and size

Create bulleted
and numbered lists

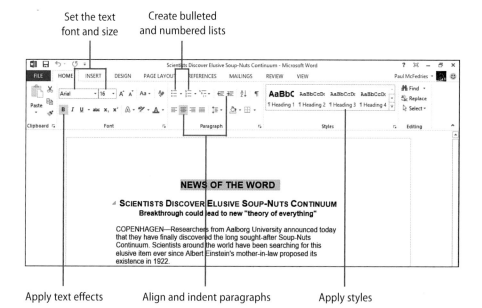

Apply text effects

Align and indent paragraphs

Apply styles

In this chapter, you'll learn various ways to format your Office RT documents, including changing the font, creating bulleted and numbered lists, and applying styles.

→ Setting the typeface, type size, and other font effects
→ Building bulleted and numbered lists
→ Working with indentation and alignment
→ Applying styles to document text
→ Copying and clearing formatting

Formatting Documents

One of the consequences of the domination enjoyed by Microsoft Office in the productivity suite market is that people—particularly businesspeople—now have high expectations. That is, because so many users have access to powerful formatting techniques, people have come to expect that the documents they read will have a relatively high level of visual appeal. Send someone a plain, unformatted memo and although they might not throw it out without a glance, they're likely to look down their noses at such a ragtag specimen. So, although you need to always ensure your content is up to snuff (accurate, grammatically correct, and so on), you also need to spend some time making sure that the content looks its best.

When you are working with formatting in the Office RT applications, it helps to remember that there are only three main types of formatting and only two main methods for applying formatting.

Here are the three main types of formatting:

- **Font formatting**—This is also called *character formatting* and it refers to attributes applied to individual characters, including the font (or typeface), type size, text effects (such as bold, italic, and underline), and text color.

- **Paragraph formatting**—This refers to attributes applied to paragraphs as a whole, including indenting, alignment, line spacing, spacing before and after the paragraph, bullets, numbering, background shading, and borders.

- **Document formatting**—This refers to attributes applied to the document as a whole, including margins, headers, footers, columns, page orientation, paper size, columns, line numbers, and hyphenation.

Here are the two main methods for applying font and paragraph formatting in the Office RT applications:

- **Directly**—With this method, you select individual font and paragraph attributes yourself. If you selected text beforehand, the application applies the formatting to the selection; otherwise, it applies the formatting to the current cursor position.

- **Styles**—A *style* is a predefined collection of formatting options. With this method, when you apply a style to text, the Office RT application applies all the style's formatting options at once. Also, if you change a formatting option within a style, all the text that uses that style is automatically updated with the new formatting. You'll find out more on this feature later in this chapter.

Selecting Text

Before you can do anything with text in the Office RT applications—that is, before you can change the font, format paragraphs, apply styles, and so on—you need to tell the application which text you want to work with. You do that by *selecting* the text, which then appears on the screen with a gray background. This applies to text in Word, PowerPoint, and OneNote, as well as to text within an Excel cell. (To learn how to select multiple Excel cells, see "Selecting a Range" in Chapter 8, "Getting More Out of Excel Ranges.")

How you select text in an Office RT application varies slightly depending on whether you're using a mouse (or trackpad) or a touchscreen.

Selecting Text with a Mouse

If you're using Office RT on a PC that has a connected mouse or trackpad, you can use that device to select text.

1. Click just slightly to the left of the first character you want to include in the selection. The insertion point appears to the left of that character.

2. Click and drag the mouse pointer to the right. As you drag the mouse, the Office RT application selects the text.

3. When you get to the last character you want to include in the selection, release the mouse. The Office RT application displays the Mini Toolbar, which you can use to format the selected text.

Mouse Text Selection Tricks

In all the Office RT applications, you can select a single word by double-clicking that word. In PowerPoint, OneNote, and Word, you can select an entire paragraph by triple-clicking anywhere inside that paragraph.

Insertion point

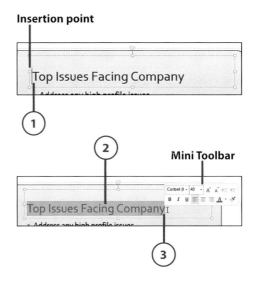

It's Not All Good

SELECTED TEXT IS EASILY DELETED TEXT

When you select text—whether it's just a few characters, a word or two, or one or more paragraphs—the Office RT applications treat that selection as a single item. That's normally a good thing because it means that when you perform an operation such as applying formatting, the application applies the format to the entire selection. On the downside, it also means that you can easily delete the selection by mistake. If you have text selected when you press a character, the application immediately deletes the selected text and replaces it with that character! So exercise a bit of caution around a keyboard while you have text selected. If you do accidentally delete the selected text, immediately click Undo in the Quick Access Toolbar or press Ctrl+Z.

Selecting Text on a Touchscreen

If you're using Office RT on a touch-screen PC, you can use gestures to select text.

1. Tap just slightly to the left of the first character you want to include in the selection. The insertion point appears to the left of that character, as does the selection handle.

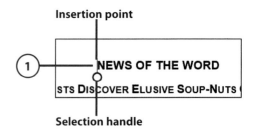

Insertion point

NEWS OF THE WORD

STS DISCOVER ELUSIVE SOUP-NUTS

Selection handle

2. Tap and drag the selection handle to the right. As you drag the handle, the Office RT application selects the text.

3. When you get to the last character you want to include in the selection, release the selection handle. You now see two selection handles, one at the beginning of the selection and one at the end.

4. If you need to adjust where the selection begins, tap and drag the start selection handle.

5. If you need to adjust where the selection ends, tap and drag the end selection handle.

6. Tap the selection. The application displays the Mini Toolbar, which you can use to format the selected text.

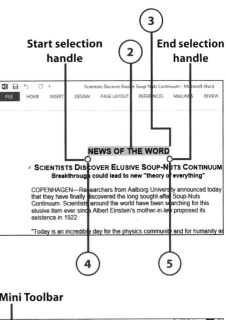

Start selection handle

End selection handle

Mini Toolbar

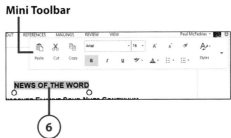

Touch Text Selection Trick

In all the Office RT applications, you can select a single word by double-tapping that word.

Changing the Font

Windows and Mac OS X have turned many otherwise ordinary citizens into avid amateur typographers. Users at cocktail parties the world over are debating the relative merits of "serif" versus "sans serif" fonts, expounding the virtues of typefaces with names like Cambria and Helvetica, and throwing around font jargon terms such as *ascender*, *feet*, and *points*. (If many, or even all, of these terms are new to you, not to worry: I explain them all in this chapter.)

Okay, so most of us don't take fonts to that extreme. However, we certainly appreciate what they do to jazz up our reports, spreadsheets, and presentations. There's nothing like a well-chosen font to add just the right tone to a document and to make our work stand out from the herd.

I always like to describe fonts as the "architecture" of characters. When you examine a building, certain features and patterns help you identify the building's architectural style. A flying buttress, for example, is usually a telltale sign of a Gothic structure. Fonts, too, are distinguished by a unique set of characteristics. Specifically, four items define the architecture of any character: typeface, type size, type effects, and type color. I discuss all four characteristics in the sections that follow and show you how to apply them using the Office RT applications.

Understanding Typefaces

A *typeface* is a distinctive design that's common to any related set of letters, numbers, and symbols. This design gives each character a particular shape and thickness (or *weight*, as it's called in type circles) that's unique to the typeface and difficult to classify. However, four main categories serve to distinguish all typefaces:

- **Serif**—A serif (rhymes with *sheriff*) typeface contains fine cross strokes (called *feet*) at the extremities of each character. These subtle appendages give the typeface a traditional, classy look that's most often used for titles and headings. The default Office RT typeface for headings, Cambria, is a serif typeface.

- **Sans serif**—A sans serif typeface doesn't contain cross strokes on the extremities of characters. As a result, sans serif typefaces usually have a cleaner, more modern look that works best for regular text. The default Office RT typeface for document text, Calibri, is a sans serif typeface.

- **Fixed-width**—A fixed-width typeface—also called a *monospace* typeface—uses the same amount of space for each character, so skinny letters such as *i* and *l* take up as much space as wider letters such as *m* and *w*. Although this is admirably egalitarian, these fonts tend to look as if they were produced with a typewriter (in other words, they're ugly). Courier New is an example of a fixed-width typeface.

- **Decorative**—Decorative typefaces are usually special designs that are supposed to convey a particular effect. So, for example, if your document needs a fancy, handwritten effect, a font like Brush Script MT is perfect.

I should also mention here that each Office RT document you work with has a theme applied. A document *theme* is a predefined collection of formatting options that you can apply all at once, just by selecting a different theme. Each theme comes with preset formatting in three categories: color scheme, font scheme, and effect scheme (which includes formatting such as drop shadows and 3-D effects).

We're talking about fonts here, so you should know that each Office RT theme comes with more than two dozen built-in font schemes that make it easy to apply fonts to your documents. Each font scheme defines two fonts: a larger font, called the *heading font*, for title and heading text; and a smaller font, called the *body font*, for regular document text. The typeface is often the same for both types of text, but some schemes use two different typefaces, such as Cambria for titles and headings and Calibri for body text.

Setting the Typeface

When setting the typeface, you can apply it either to existing text or to text that you're about to add to the document.

1. Select the text you want to format. Or, if you want to format the next text you type, position the cursor where you want the text to appear.

2. Select the Home tab.

3. Drop down the Font list.

4. Select the typeface you want to use. The Office RT application applies the typeface to the text.

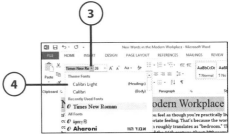

Changing the Type Size

You can use type sizes to gain more control over the display of a document. For example, if you want to emphasize a title or heading, you can increase the type size. Similarly, if you want to fit more text into a particular area—such as a worksheet cell or a PowerPoint text box—you can decrease the type size.

1. Select the text you want to format. Or, if you want to format the next text you type, position the cursor where you want the text to appear.

2. Select the Home tab.

3. Drop down the Font Size list.

4. Select the type size you want to use. The Office RT application applies the type size to the text.

Keyboard Shortcut

Press Ctrl+Shift+> to increase the type size by two points; press Ctrl+Shift+< to decrease the type size by two points. In Word, you can also press Ctrl+] to increase the type size by one point and Ctrl+[to decrease the type size by one point.

Select Increase Font to increase the type size by two points

Select Decrease Font to decrease the type size by two points

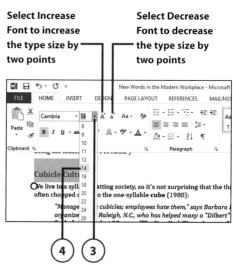

>>>Go Further

UNDERSTANDING TYPE SIZE

The *type size* measures the height of a font. The standard unit of measurement is the *point*, where there are 72 points in one inch. So, for example, the letters in a 24-point font are twice as tall as those in a 12-point font. Technically, type size is measured from the highest point of any letter with an *ascender*, which is the top part of a letter that extends above the letter body (such as the lowercase *f* and *h*), to the lowest point of a letter with a *descender*, which is the bottom part a letter that extends below the letter baseline (such as the lowercase *g* or *y*). (In case you're wondering, this book is laid out in a 10-point Myriad Pro font.)

Applying Type Effects

The *type effects* of a font refer to extra attributes added to the typeface, such as **bold** and *italic*. Other type effects (often called type *styles*) include <u>underline</u> and ~~strikethrough~~. You normally use these styles to highlight or add emphasis to text.

1. Select the text you want to format. Or, if you want to format the next text you type, position the cursor where you want the text to appear.

2. Select the Home tab.

3. Use the icons to select the type effects you want to apply.

4. If you don't see the effect you want, select the Font group dialog box launcher. The Font dialog box opens.

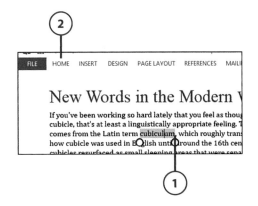

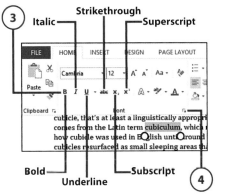

5. Select the Font tab.

6. Use the Font Style list to apply bold, italic, or both.

7. Use the Underline Style list to apply an underline effect.

8. Use the Effects check boxes to apply other effects.

9. Select OK. The Office RT application applies the type effects to the text.

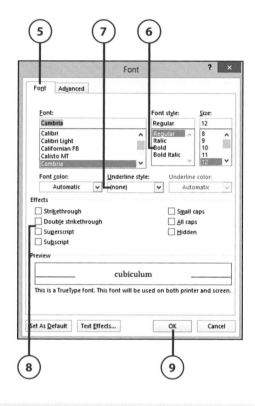

KEYBOARD SHORTCUTS

The Office RT applications offer a number of shortcuts for applying text effects:

Press	To do the following
Ctrl+B	Apply bold
Ctrl+I	Apply italic
Ctrl+U	Apply underline
Ctrl+Shift+D	Apply double underline
Ctrl+Shift+W	Apply underline to each word in the selection (Word only)
Ctrl+=	Apply subscript
Ctrl++	Apply superscript
Ctrl+D	Display the Font dialog box with the Font tab selected

>>>Go Further

Setting Text Colors

You can add some visual interest to your documents by changing the color of the document text. In most cases, you'll want to set the color of just the text itself. However, in Word and OneNote, you can also highlight sections of a document by applying a color to the text background. As with fonts, the colors you have available in Word, Excel, and PowerPoint depend on the theme applied to the document: Each theme comes with a palette of 60 colors. However, you can also choose a color from the application's palette of 10 standard colors.

1. Select the text you want to format. Or, if you want to format the next text you type, position the cursor where you want the text to appear.

2. Select the Home tab.

3. Drop down the Font Color list.

4. Select the color you want to apply.

5. In Word and OneNote, you can also use the Text Highlight Color list to apply a highlight to the text.

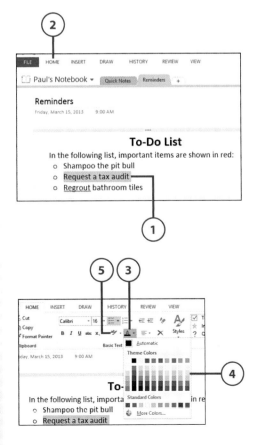

>>>Go Further

GETTING CREATIVE WITH A CUSTOM COLOR

The 60 theme colors and 10 standard colors seem like large palette, but you might not find the color that's just right for your needs. In that case, you take matters into your own hands and create the color you want. In the Font Color list, select More Colors to display the Colors dialog box. Select the Custom tab and then either click a color in the spectrum provided or use the Red, Green, and Blue spin boxes to specify exact color values between 0 and 255 for each color. A lower number means the color is less intense and a higher number means the color is more intense.

Alternatively, select HSL in the Color Model list and then enter values in the Hue, Sat, and Lum spin boxes. With this method, you're setting three different attributes: hue, saturation, and luminance. Hue (which is more or less equivalent to the term *color*) measures the position on the color spectrum. Lower numbers indicate a position near the red end, and higher numbers move through the yellow, green, blue, and violet parts of the spectrum. Saturation is a measure of the purity of a given hue, where a setting of 240 means that the hue is a pure color and lower numbers indicate that more gray is mixed with the hue. Luminance is a measure of the brightness of a color, where lower numbers are darker and higher numbers are brighter.

Formatting Paragraphs

The Word, PowerPoint, and OneNote applications are simple programs in the sense that it's easy to get started with them: You just create a new document or open an existing document and then start typing. Of course, not all documents consist of basic text. For example, you might require a bulleted or numbered list, or you might need to adjust the indentation or alignment of a paragraph. This section shows you how to perform these tasks in the Word, PowerPoint, and OneNote applications.

Building a Bulleted List

You can make a list of items more prominent and more readable by formatting those items as a bulleted list. When you do, the application formats the items slightly indented from the regular text, with a small character—called the bullet, which is usually a black dot—in front of each item.

You can either create a bulleted list from scratch or convert an existing list of items to a bulleted list. You also have a choice of several different bullet characters.

1. If you want to convert existing text to a bulleted list, select the text.

Converting Text to a Bulleted List

If you're selecting text to convert to a bulleted list, the text must be a series of items, of any length, each in its own paragraph.

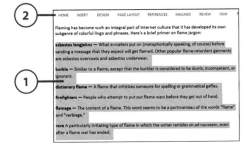

2. Select the Home tab.

3. Select Bullets. If you selected your text in advance, the application converts the text to a bulleted list.

4. To choose a different bullet style, drop down the Bullets list and then select a bullet style.

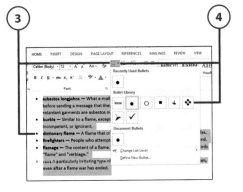

5. If you selected text in advance, click or tap at the end of the last item. The insertion point moves to the end of the item.

6. Press Enter. The application creates a new item in the bulleted list.

7. Type the text for the new list item.

8. Repeat steps 6 and 7 until you complete the bulleted list.

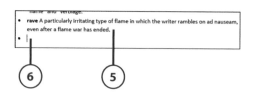

Creating Subbullets

If you want to shift a list item so that it's a subbullet of the item above it, click or tap at the beginning of the item and then press Tab. To return the item to its previous level, press Shift+Tab.

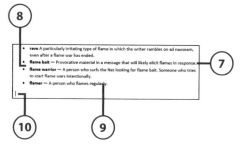

9. Click or tap at the end of the last item.

10. Press Enter twice. The application ends the bulleted list.

DEFINING YOUR OWN BULLETS

The Office RT applications offer a few different bullet styles, but nothing that's all that creative or interesting. To add some pizzazz to your document, you can define your own bullet style in Word and PowerPoint.

In Word, drop down the Bullets list and select Define New Bullet to open the Define New Bullet dialog box. You now have three choices: Select Symbol to open the Symbol dialog box and choose a character as your bullet style, select Picture to open the Insert Pictures dialog box and choose an image as your bullet style, or select Font to open the Font dialog box and choose a typeface such as Wingdings to render the current bullet style with a different font.

In PowerPoint, drop down the Bullets list and select Bullets and Numbering to open the Bullets and Numbering dialog box. Select Picture to choose an image as the bullet or Customize to choose a character as the bullet.

Creating a Numbered List

You can make a set of steps or an ordered list more readable and easier to follow by formatting those items as a numbered list. When you do, the application formats the items slightly indented from the regular text, with a number in front of each item. The numbers increase sequentially, usually from 1 to the total number of items in the list.

You can either create a numbered list from scratch or convert an existing list of items to a numbered list. You also have a choice of several different numbering characters.

1. If you want to convert existing text to a numbered list, select the text.

Converting Text to a Numbered List

If you're selecting text to convert to a numbered list, the text must be a series of items, of any length, each in its own paragraph.

2. Select the Home tab.

3. Select Numbering. If you selected your text in advance, the application converts the text to a numbered list.

4. To choose a different number format, drop down the Numbering list and then select a format.

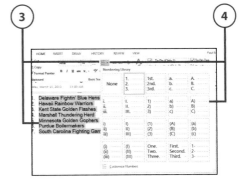

5. If you selected the text in advance, click or tap at the end of the last item. The insertion point moves to the end of the item.

6. Press Enter. The application creates a new item in the numbered list.

7. Type the text for the new list item.

8. Repeat steps 6 and 7 until you complete the numbered list.

9. Click or tap at the end of the last item.

10. Press Enter twice. The application ends the numbered list.

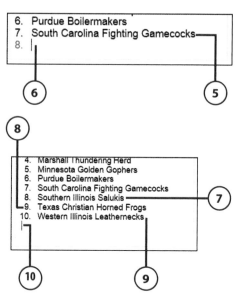

DEFINING YOUR OWN NUMBERS

Office RT offers only a few numbering formats, but you can define your own number format in Word, OneNote, and PowerPoint.

In Word, drop down the Numbering list and select Define New Number Format to open the Define New Number Format dialog box. Select an item from the Number Style list, and then use the Font button and the Number Format text box to customize the style.

In OneNote, drop down the Numbering list and select Customize Numbers to open the Customize Numbering task pane. Use the Sequence and Format lists to set the number style you want to use.

In PowerPoint, drop down the Numbering list and select Bullets and Numbering to open the Bullets and Numbering dialog box. On the Numbered tab, select a style and then customize its size and color.

>>>Go Further

Setting the Indentation

You can set a paragraph off from the rest of the text by indenting the paragraph. For example, if a document includes a lengthy quotation, you can indent the quotation to make it stand out. In the Word, PowerPoint, and OneNote applications, you can indent a paragraph from the left.

1. Click or tap inside the paragraph you want to indent. If you want to indent multiple paragraphs, select some or all of the text in each of the paragraphs.

2. Select the Home tab.

3. Select Increase Indent. The application shifts the entire paragraph away from the left margin.

4. Repeat step 3 until the paragraph is indented the amount you want. If you indent a paragraph too much, you can shift the text back toward the left margin by clicking Decrease Indent.

Keyboard Shortcut

In Word, you can also increase the indent by pressing Ctrl+M and you can decrease the indent by pressing Ctrl+Shift+M.

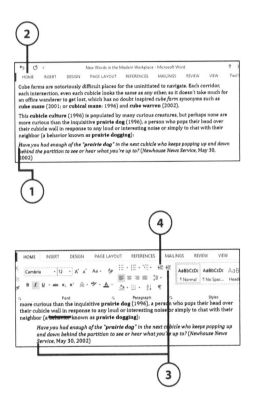

Aligning Paragraphs

You can make a document easier to read by aligning its text horizontally. You can align the text with the left margin (this is the default alignment), with the right margin, or with the center of the document. In Word, you can also justify a paragraph's text, which means the text gets aligned with both the left and right margins.

You can apply these alignments to one or more paragraphs in a Word application document, to one or more cells in an Excel application worksheet, to text in a PowerPoint application slide, or to paragraphs in a OneNote application page.

1. Click or tap inside the paragraph or cell you want to align. If you want to align multiple items, select some or all of the text in each of the paragraphs or select each cell.

2. Select the Home tab.

3. Select the icon for the alignment you want to apply.

Keyboard Shortcut

The Word, PowerPoint, and OneNote applications offer keyboard shortcuts for aligning paragraphs: Ctrl+L for align text left, Ctrl+E for center, and Ctrl+R for align text right. In Word, you can also press Ctrl+J to justify text.

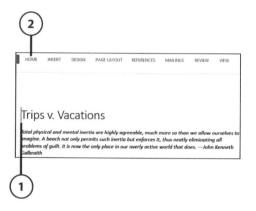

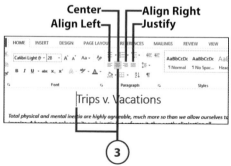

Working with Formatting

Working with text and paragraph formatting can be time consuming and labor intensive. It's almost always worth the extra effort to make your Office documents look their best, but that doesn't mean you should waste time performing your formatting chores. The Office RT applications offer a few handy features that can help reduce the amount of time and effort you expend on your formatting, and the rest of this chapter covers these useful tools.

Applying Styles

You can save time and effort when formatting your documents by taking advantage of the predefined styles that are available in the Office RT applications. A *style* is a collection of formatting options, usually including some or all of the following: typeface, type size, text color, text effects, and paragraph alignment. When you apply a style to some text, the application applies all of the style's formatting at once.

The Office RT applications offer a large number of predefined styles, the look of which depends on the document theme.

1. Select the text you want to format.

2. Select the Home tab.

3. In Word and OneNote, select More Styles to display the gallery of predefined styles. In Excel, select Cell Styles; in PowerPoint, select Quick Styles.

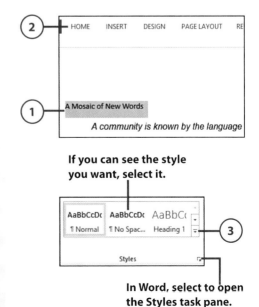

If you can see the style you want, select it.

In Word, select to open the Styles task pane.

4. Click the style you want to use. The Office application applies the style's formatting to the text.

Word's Complete Style List

In Word, the Styles gallery only shows a partial list of styles. To see the full list, either select the Styles dialog box launcher or press Ctrl+Alt+Shift+S. Word displays the Styles task pane, which contains the complete list of available styles.

Copying Formatting

It can take a fair amount of work to get some text or a paragraph formatted just right. That's bad enough, but things get worse if you then have to repeat the entire procedure for another selection. The more times you have to repeat a format, the less likely you are to begin the whole process in the first place.

Fortunately, the Office RT applications have an underappreciated tool that can remove almost all the drudgery from applying the same formatting to multiple selections. It's called the Format Painter tool and you can use it to copy the formatting from some existing text to another selection.

1. Select the text that has the formatting you want to copy. If you're copying formatting from regular text or a paragraph, you need only click or tap within that text.

2. Select the Home tab.

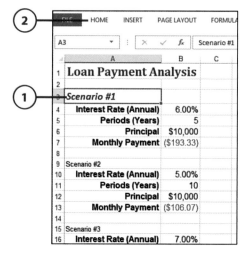

3. Double-click the Format Painter tool. If you only need to copy the formatting once, just click the Format Painter tool.

4. Click the text or paragraph that you want to receive the formatting. The application transfers the formatting from the selected text to the new text.

5. If you double-clicked Format Painter, repeat step 4 for each of the other areas that you want to format.

6. If you double-clicked Format Painter, click the button once more to turn off the feature.

Clearing Formatting

If you apply a number of font formats, paragraph options, or styles to some text, you might decide later that you no longer want any of that formatting. Although it's possible to turn off or remove each of the formatting options individually, the Office RT applications offer a much easier method: the Clear Formatting command. Selecting this command removes all formatting from the selected text, so this method is much easier than trying to clear the formatting options one by one.

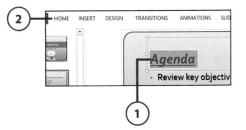

1. Select the text you want to clear.

2. Select the Home tab.

3. Select Clear Formatting. In Excel, drop down the Clear list and then select Clear Formats. The Office application clears all formatting from the text.

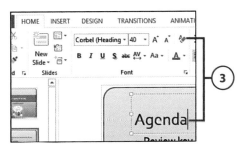

Apply picture
styles

Apply picture
effects

Rotate a
graphic

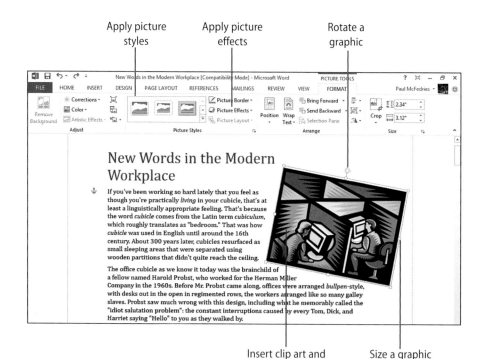

Insert clip art and
other images

Size a graphic

In this chapter, you'll learn various techniques for drawing, inserting, and working with graphic objects, such as lines, photos, and clip art.

→ Drawing lines, rectangles, and circles
→ Inserting photos, clip art, SmartArt graphics, and WordArt images
→ Selecting one or more graphic objects
→ Sizing, moving, and rotating graphic objects
→ Applying styles and effects to graphic objects

Working with Office RT Graphics

When most people think about using the Office RT applications, they generally think about text, whether it is writing sentences and paragraphs in Word, adding formulas and labels in Excel, creating slide titles and bullets in PowerPoint, and so on. It is certainly true that most of the work people do in Office RT—from papers to purchase orders to presentations—is and should remain text based.

However, if you *only* think text when you think of Office, you're missing out on a whole other dimension. All the Office RT applications have extensive graphics tools that you can take advantage of to improve the clarity of your work or just to add a bit of pizzazz to liven up an otherwise drab document.

Even better, these graphics tools work the same across applications, so once you learn how to use them, you can apply your knowledge to any program. This chapter shows you how to create, edit, and enhance graphics in the Office RT applications.

Working with Shapes

A shape is an object such as a line or rectangle that you draw within your document. You can use shapes to point out key features in a document, enclose text, create flowcharts, and enhance the look of a document. In Office RT, you can use eight shape types:

- **Lines**—Straight lines, squiggles, free-form polygons, arrows, connectors, and curves

- **Basic Shapes**—Rectangles, triangles, circles, boxes, cylinders, hearts, and many more

- **Block Arrows**—Two-dimensional arrows of various configurations

- **Equation Shapes**—Two-dimensional images for the basic arithmetic symbols, such as plus (+) and equals (=)

- **Flowchart**—The standard shapes used for creating flowcharts

- **Callouts**—Boxes and lines for creating callouts to document features

- **Stars and Banners**—Stars, starbursts, scrolls, and more

- **Action Buttons (PowerPoint only)**—Buttons such as forward and backward that represent standard slide show actions

Inserting a Line

You can use lines to point out important document information, create
a free-form drawing, or as part of
a more complex graphic, such as a
company logo.

1. Select the Insert tab. In OneNote,
   select the Draw tab, instead.

2. Select Shapes and then select the
   shape you want from the Lines
   section.

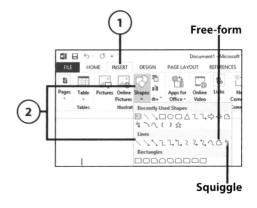

3. On a touchscreen, position a finger or stylus where you want to begin the line. If you're using a mouse, position the crosshair where you want to start drawing the line.

4. Drag to where you want the line to end and then release. If you're drawing a squiggle, drag in the shape of the line you want.

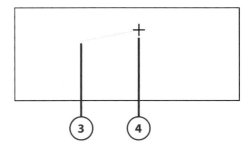

Taming Your Lines

If you have a keyboard, you can restrict straight lines and arrows to horizontal, vertical, and 45-degree angles by holding down the Shift key while you drag the screen.

DRAWING A FREE-FORM POLYGON

The Lines section of the Shapes gallery includes a Free-Form icon that enables you to draw a free-form polygon, which is really just a series of connected lines that create a closed shape. To draw a free-form polygon, follow steps 1 to 4 to create the first side of the shape. Then, using a stylus or mouse (this doesn't work with a finger, unfortunately), tap where you want each subsequent side to end. When you're done, double-tap the screen.

>>> Go Further

Inserting Any Other Shape

You can use the other shapes either on their own—for example, to point out features with callouts or block arrows or to enhance text with stars or banners—or as part of a more complex graphic.

1. Select the Insert tab. In OneNote, select the Draw tab, instead.

2. Select Shapes and then select the shape you want to insert.

3. On a touchscreen, position your finger or stylus where you want to begin the shape. If you're using a mouse, position the crosshair where you want to start drawing the shape.

4. Drag until the shape has the size and form you want and then release.

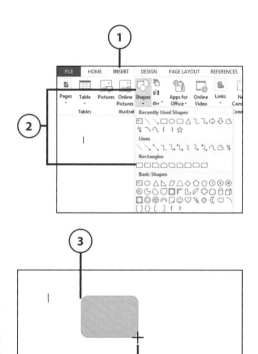

Drawing Squares and Circles

If you have a keyboard, you can make your rectangles square, your ellipses circular, and your angled lines 45 degrees, by holding down the Shift key while you drag the screen.

Inserting Images

Although the shape tools that come with the Office RT applications are handy for creating simple graphics effects, your document might require something more ambitious or specific. Office RT can help here, too, by offering several types of images that you can insert:

- **Picture**—You can enhance the visual appeal and strengthen the message of a document by adding a picture to the file. The Office RT applications can work with the most popular picture formats, including BMP, JPEG, TIFF, PNG, and GIF. This means that you can insert almost any photo that you have stored on your computer.

- **Clip art**—This refers to small images or artwork that you can insert into your documents. Office RT doesn't come with its own clip art, but it does give you access to the online Office.com clip art collection, which contains thousands of images from various categories, such as business, people, nature, and symbols. You can use any of these clip art images without charge.

- **SmartArt**—You use these graphics to help present information in a compact, visual format. A SmartArt graphic is a collection of *nodes*— shapes with some text inside—that enables you to convey information visually. For example, you can use a SmartArt graphic to present a company organization chart, the progression of steps in a workflow, the parts that make up a whole, and much more.

- **Text box**—The graphics you add to your documents will usually consist of images, but times will occur when you need to augment those images with some text. For example, you might want to add a title and subtitle or insert a label. To add text to an existing image, you draw a text box and then type your text within that box.

- **WordArt**—You can add some pizzazz to your documents by inserting a WordArt image, which is a graphic object that contains text stylized with shadows, outlines, reflections, and other predefined effects. WordArt images enable you to apply sophisticated and fun effects to text with just a few taps. However, some of the more elaborate WordArt effects can make text difficult to read, so make sure that whatever WordArt image you use does not detract from your document message.

Inserting a Picture

If you have a photo or other image on your computer that you think would add just the right touch, you can insert it into your document.

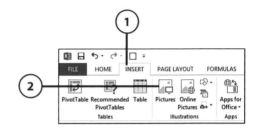

1. Select the Insert tab.

2. Select Pictures to open the Insert Picture dialog box.

3. Open the folder that contains the picture you want to insert.

4. Select the picture.

5. Select Insert. The Office RT application inserts the picture into the document.

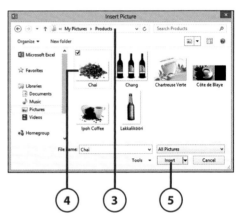

LINKING TO THE PICTURE

You can set up a link between the inserted picture and the original file, so that any changes you make to the original are automatically reflected in the document copy. Follow steps 1 to 4 to select the picture in the Insert Picture dialog box, then drop down the Insert menu.

If you want to keep your document size small, select Link to File to insert the picture as a link to the original file. Use this command when you want edits to the original file to be updated in your document but you don't want a copy of the picture in the document. Note, however, that if you send the file to someone (say, via email or over a network), that person will not see the image unless he or she has the same image located in the same folder.

Alternatively, select Insert and Link to insert a copy of the picture into the document *and* maintain a link to the original file. Use this command when you want edits to the original file to be updated in your document but you also want a copy within the document just in case the original is deleted.

Inserting Clip Art

Clip art is professional-quality artwork that can often add just the right
touch to a newsletter, brochure, or
presentation, and Office.com offers
a huge selection of clip art images in
dozens of different categories.

1. Select the Insert tab.

2. Select Online Pictures to open the
   Insert Pictures dialog box.

3. Type a word that describes the
   type of clip art image you want to
   insert.

4. Select Search. The application
   displays a list of clip art images
   that match your search term.

More Online Images

To search for an image on the
Web, use the Bing Image Search
option to search for the picture.
If you have connected your Flickr
account to Windows RT, you
can also use the Flickr option to
choose a photo. If you are using a
Microsoft account with Windows
RT, you can use the SkyDrive
option to select an image from
your SkyDrive.

5. Select the clip art image you want
   to use.

6. Select Insert. The Office RT application inserts the clip art into the
   document.

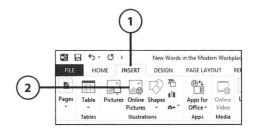

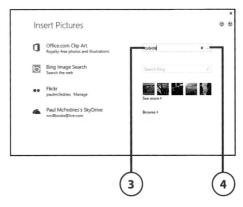

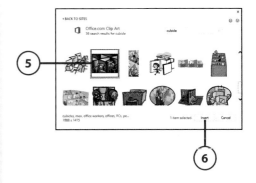

>>>Go Further

CLIP ART DIRECT FROM THE SOURCE

If you'd like an even easier way to locate the clip art image that you want, you can use a web browser to locate clip art images directly using the Office.com website. Navigate to http://office.microsoft.com/en-us/images/ and then select an image category, such as Business or People. Next, filter the images by media type and image size. For clip art, you should select Illustration in the Media Type list and All in the Image Size list.

Understanding SmartArt Graphics

One of the most impressive of the Office RT graphics features is support for the SmartArt format, which is based on the XML (Extensible Markup Language) standard. A SmartArt graphic is a collection of *nodes*—shapes with some text inside—that enables you to convey information visually. You use SmartArt to illustrate concepts in seven main categories:

- **List**—These are concepts that are sequential or that form a progression or a group. Most of these SmartArt graphics consist of shapes arranged in vertical or horizontal lists.

- **Process**—These are concepts that progress from one stage to another, where the overall progress has a beginning and an end. In most of these SmartArt graphics, each stage is represented by a shape and accompanying text, and one-way arrows lead you from one shape to the next.

- **Cycle**—These are concepts that progress from one stage to another in a repeating pattern. In most of these SmartArt graphics, each stage is represented by a shape and accompanying text, and one-way arrows lead you from one shape to the next. The most common structure is a circle, with the last stage leading back to the first stage.

- **Hierarchy**—These are concepts that either show the relative importance of one thing over another, or show how one thing is contained within another. These SmartArt graphics look like organization charts.

- **Relationship**—These are concepts that show how two or more items are connected to each other. In most of these SmartArt graphics, each item is represented by a shape and accompanying text, and all the shapes either reside within a larger structure, such as a pyramid, or are positioned relative to one another, such as in a Venn diagram.

- **Matrix**—These are concepts that show the relationship between the entirety of something and its components, organized as quadrants. These SmartArt graphics have one shape that represents the whole and four shapes that represent the component quadrants.

- **Pyramid**—These are concepts with components that are proportional to each other or interconnected in some way. In most of these SmartArt graphics, the component shapes are arranged in a triangle pattern.

Inserting a SmartArt Graphic

To build a SmartArt graphic, you use the Text pane to add text to each node as well as add and delete nodes.

1. Select the Insert tab.

2. Select SmartArt to open the Choose a SmartArt Graphic dialog box.

3. Select a SmartArt category.

4. Select the SmartArt style you want to use.

5. Select OK to add the SmartArt graphic to the document.

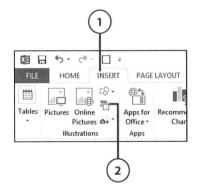

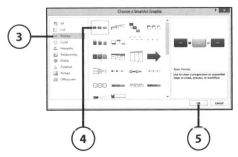

6. Select a node in the Text pane and then type the text that you want to appear in the node.

7. Repeat step 6 to fill in the other nodes in the SmartArt graphic.

8. To add a node to the SmartArt graphic, select the existing node you want the new node to come before or after.

9. Select the Design tab.

10. Select Add Shape and then select either Add Shape After or Add Shape Before.

Deleting Nodes

To remove a node from the SmartArt graphic, tap and hold (or right-click) the node for a few seconds, then select Cut in the shortcut menu that appears.

Select Text Pane to toggle the Text pane on and off.

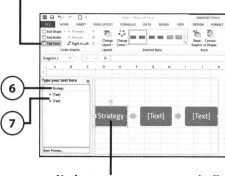

Node text appears automatically in the associated shape.

Use the Format tab to customize specific shapes.

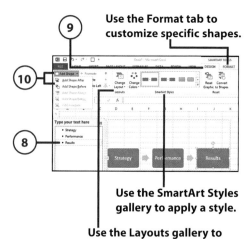

Use the SmartArt Styles gallery to apply a style.

Use the Layouts gallery to choose a different layout.

Inserting WordArt

WordArt takes a word or phrase and converts it into a graphic object that applies artistic styles, colors, and shapes to the text. WordArt is therefore useful for newsletter titles, logos, and any time you want text to really stand out from its surroundings.

1. Select the Insert tab.

2. Select WordArt to open the WordArt gallery.

3. Select the WordArt style you want to use. The Office RT application adds the WordArt image to the document.

4. Type the text that you want to appear in the WordArt image.

5. Tap outside the image to set it.

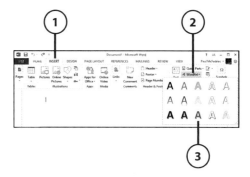

Use the Shape Styles gallery and commands to customize the image.

Use the WordArt Styles gallery to apply a style.

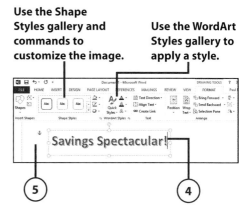

Savings Spectacular!

ADDING A TEXT BOX

The graphics you add to your documents will usually consist of images, but sometimes you'll need to augment those images with text. For example, you might want to add a title and subtitle or insert a label. If a WordArt image seems like overkill for this, then a better alternative is to draw a text box and then type your text within that box.

To add a text box, select Insert, Text Box, use a finger or stylus to drag until the text box has the size and form you want, and then type your text in the box.

>>>Go Further

Formatting and Editing Graphic Objects

Inserting a line, shape, picture, or other graphic object is usually only half the battle. To complete your work with the graphic, you usually need to spend a bit of time formatting and editing the object to get it just right. This may include some or all of the following: sizing the graphic; rotating it; moving it; grouping or aligning it with other objects; and formatting the object's fill, lines, and shadow effects. The rest of this chapter provides you with the details of these and other techniques for working with graphics objects.

Selecting Graphic Objects

Every graphic object has an invisible rectangular frame. For a line or rectangle, the frame is the same as the object itself. For all other objects, the frame is a rectangle that completely encloses the shape or image. Before you can format or edit a graphic object, you must select it, which displays selection handles around the frame.

If you just want to work with a single object, then you can select it by tapping it. If you need to work with multiple objects, Office RT gives you a number of methods and the one you choose depends on the number of objects and their layout within the document:

- The simplest scenario is when you have just a few objects to select. In this case, hold down the Ctrl key and tap each object. If you tap an object by accident, keep the Ctrl key held down and tap the object again to deselect it.

- To select a few objects, you can "lasso" the objects, as described in the next section.

- To select all the objects in a document, select one and then press Ctrl+A.

Lassoing Graphic Objects

Lassoing graphic objects begins using a finger or stylus to draw a rectangle around the objects you want to select. Use this technique when the objects you want are located near each other.

1. Select the Home tab.

2. Tap Select.

3. Tap Select Objects.

Lassoing Objects in Excel

To lasso objects in Excel, select the Home tab, then Find & Select, then Select Objects.

---

4. Place a finger or stylus at the upper-left corner of the area you want to select.

5. Tap and drag to the lower-right corner of the area you want to select. As you drag, the program indicates the selected area with a dashed border.

6. When the selection area completely encloses each object you want to select, release the screen. Excel places selection handles around each object in the selection area.

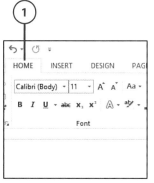

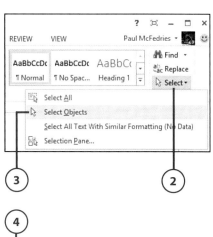

Sizing a Graphic Object

If a graphic is too large or too small for your needs, or if the object's shape is not what you want, you can size the image to change its dimensions or its shape. You might want to size a graphic so that it fits within an open document area.

1. Select the graphic you want to size.

2. To adjust the width of the graphic, drag the left or right handle.

3. To adjust the height of the graphic, drag the top or bottom handle.

4. To adjust the width and height at the same time, drag a corner handle.

Sizing handles appear around the edges of a selected object.

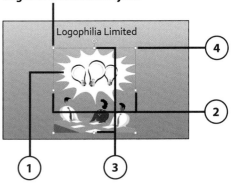

Sizing Multiple Sides

To size the graphic on all four sides at once, hold down Ctrl while you drag any corner handle. Similarly, you can size the left and right sides simultaneously by holding down Ctrl while dragging a side handle; you can size the top and bottom sides simultaneously by holding down Ctrl while dragging the top or bottom handle.

Moving a Graphic Object

To ensure that a graphic is ideally placed within a document, you can move the graphic to a new location. For example, you might want to move a graphic so that it does not cover existing document text.

1. Select the graphic you want to move.

2. Place a finger or the stylus in the middle of the object. Make sure you don't place your finger or stylus over any of the object's sizing handles.

3. Drag the object to the position you want.

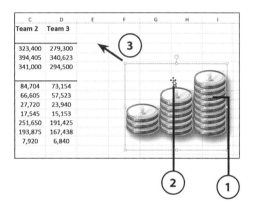

Horizontal or Vertical Moves

To move a graphic object only horizontally or vertically, hold down the Shift key while dragging it.

Rotating a Graphic Object

Most graphic objects get inserted into a document without any rotation: Horizontal borders appear horizontal, and vertical borders appear vertical. A nonrotated image is probably what you will want most of the time, but for some occasions an image tilted at a jaunty angle is just the right touch for a document. Many objects come with a rotation handle that you can use to rotate the object clockwise or counterclockwise.

1. Select the graphic you want to rotate.

2. Use a finger or stylus to drag the rotation handle. Drag the handle clockwise to rotate the graphic clockwise; drag the handle counterclockwise to rotate the graphic counterclockwise.

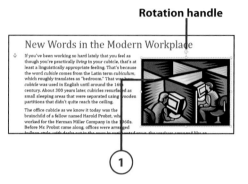

Formatting a Graphic Object

You can enhance your shapes, clip art, photos, WordArt images, and SmartArt graphics by formatting the images. For example, the Office RT applications offer more than two dozen picture styles, which are predefined formats that apply various combinations of shadows, reflections, borders, and layouts. Office RT also offers a dozen picture effects, which are preset combinations of special effects, such as glows, soft edges, bevels, and 3-D rotations.

1. Select the picture you want to format.

2. Select the Format tab.

3. Select More Picture Styles. The Picture Styles gallery appears.

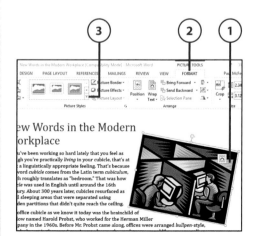

Picture Style Preview

If you're using a mouse, you can get a preview of what the style's effect will be on your graphic by hovering the mouse pointer over the style.

4. Select the picture style you want to use. The application applies the Quick Style to the picture.

5. Select Picture Effects. If the image is a shape, select Shape Effects, instead.

6. Select Preset.

7. Select the effect you want to apply. The application applies the effect to the picture.

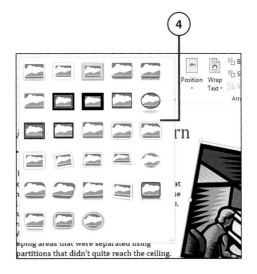

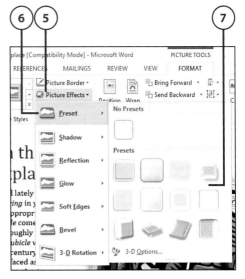

MORE EFFECTS

To gain maximum control over your graphic effects, select the object and then select Picture Effects (or Shape Effects). You can then use the six effect categories—Shadow, Reflection, Glow, Soft Edges, Bevel, and 3-D Rotation—to apply specific effects to the image.

It's Not All Good

REVERTING TO THE ORIGINAL

After playing around with a graphic for a bit, you might end up with a bit of a mess. If you don't like the formatting that you've applied to a graphic, you might prefer to return the picture to its original look and start over. If you haven't performed any other tasks since applying the formatting, select Undo (or press Ctrl+Z) until the application has removed the formatting. Otherwise, select the Format tab, select Picture Effects (or Shape Effects), select Preset, and then select the icon in the No Presets section. To reverse all the changes you've made to a picture since you inserted the image, select the picture, select Format, and then select Reset Picture.

Set tabs

Apply headings

Find text

Replace text

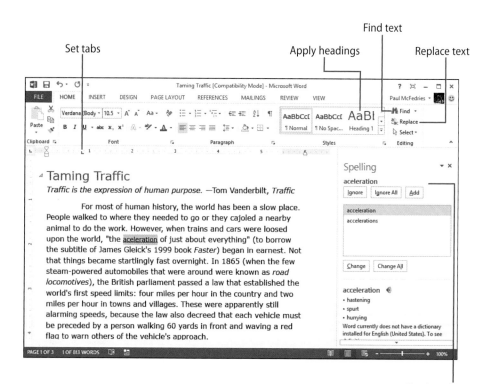

Check spelling
and grammar

In this chapter, you'll learn about working with text in Word, including entering and editing text, inserting symbols and tabs, and checking your work for spelling and grammatical mistakes.

→ Entering and editing Word text

→ Inserting foreign characters and other symbols

→ Adding tabs and headings

→ Finding and replacing document text

→ Checking for spelling and grammar errors

Working with Text in Word

All the Office RT applications require at least some written input. From worksheet titles and labels in Excel to slide headings and bullets in PowerPoint to page snippets and lists in OneNote, you always end up working with text in one form or another when you work with Office RT. However, when you have some *real* writing to do, the Office RT tool of choice is, of course, Word and its word processing pedigree. Whether you're firing off a 3-page memo to the troops or putting together a 300-page book, Word can handle any text task you throw at it.

Word is loaded with useful and powerful features that can help you not only to create beautiful documents, but also to create those documents in record time. The next few chapters are designed to introduce you to these features and other techniques for getting the most out of Word. This chapter gets you off to a good start by examining a number of handy and powerful techniques for entering and editing text in Word.

Learning Text Basics

Fritterware refers to software programs that contain so many bells and whistles that you can't help but fritter away huge amounts of time trying out different options and features. Word is a big, complex program, so it certainly qualifies as fritterware, particularly when it comes to formatting your work. Even so, you still probably spend the bulk of your Word time entering text, which means you can become immediately more productive if you learn a few techniques for making text entry easier and faster. The next few sections help you do just that.

Entering and Editing Text

You can use your Windows RT device's onscreen keyboard to enter and edit text in the Office RT applications.

The insertion point shows where the next character you type will appear.

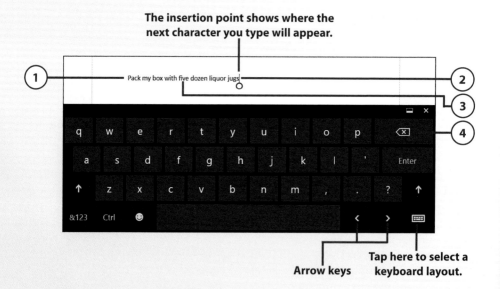

Pack my box with five dozen liquor jugs

Arrow keys   **Tap here to select a keyboard layout.**

1. Double-tap at the spot where you want to start entering text. If the document already contains text, tap at the spot where you want your next typing to appear.

2. Type your text.

3. To edit text, tap at the spot where you want to make your changes, or use the arrow keys to position the insertion point.

4. Tap Backspace to delete the character to the left of the insertion point.

UPGRADING YOUR KEYBOARD

If you plan on doing a lot of typing using Windows RT's onscreen keyboard, consider dumping the default keyboard layout in favor of the standard keyboard, which includes useful text entry and editing keys, such as Tab, Caps Lock, Delete, Up Arrow, and Down Arrow.

To make this keyboard available, swipe left from the right edge of the screen, tap Settings, and then tap Change PC Settings. In the PC Settings app, tap General and then tap the Make the Standard Keyboard Layout Available switch to On. The next time the keyboard is onscreen, tap the Keyboard icon in the lower-right corner and then tap the icon for the standard keyboard.

Entering Text with AutoCorrect

AutoCorrect is a feature that watches what you type and automatically corrects certain mistakes, such as *teh* (instead of *the*) and *wold* (instead of *would*). If you disagree with a correction, either press Ctrl+Z to undo it or select the correction and then select Change Back to "*text*," where *text* is the uncorrected version of the text.

However, most of us have phrases, sentences, even multiple paragraphs that we add to our documents regularly. Such frequently used bits of text are called *boilerplate*, and having to type them constantly can be both tedious and time wasting. To reduce the drudgery of boilerplate, you can set up AutoCorrect to store the boilerplate and then recall it with a few keystrokes.

1. Select the boilerplate text.

2. Select File.

3. Select Options to display the Word Options dialog box.

4. Select Proofing.

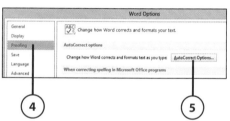

5. Select AutoCorrect Options to display the AutoCorrect dialog box.

6. Select the AutoCorrect tab.

7. If the boilerplate is formatted and you want to include that formatting each time you insert the boilerplate, select the Formatted Text option; otherwise, select the Plain Text option.

8. In the Replace text box, type a short abbreviation or code.

9. Select Add.

10. Select OK.

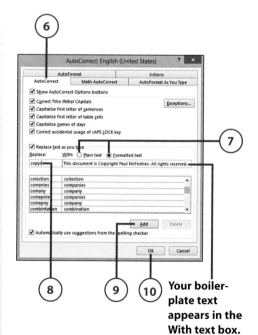

Your boilerplate text appears in the With text box.

Inserting Symbols

A Word document does not have to consist solely of those letters, numbers, punctuation marks, and other characters that you can see on your keyboard. In fact, hundreds of other symbols are available to you. These include financial symbols such as €, £, and ¥; business symbols such as ®, ™, and ©; mathematical symbols such as ≤, ∞, and ±; and international characters such as Á, ö, and ĉ.

1. Position the insertion point where you want the symbol to appear.

2. Select the Insert tab.

3. Select Symbol.

4. If you see the symbol you want to insert, select it. Otherwise, select More Symbols to open the Symbol dialog box.

5. If you want to insert the symbol using a particular font, select the font you want in the Font list.

6. Select the symbol you want to insert.

7. Select Insert. Word inserts the symbol at the insertion point.

Shortcut

You can also double-tap the symbol to enter it.

8. Select Close.

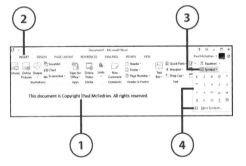

Select this tab to see a list of commonly used symbols

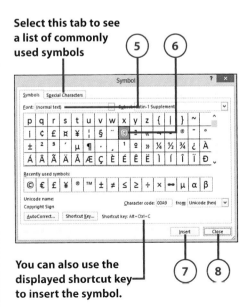

You can also use the displayed shortcut key to insert the symbol.

CREATING AN AUTOCORRECT ENTRY FOR A SYMBOL

As you see in the next section, Word has a few predefined AutoCorrect entries for symbols. If you have other symbols that you use more often, you can insert them via the convenience of AutoCorrect.

In the Symbol dialog box, select the symbol you want to work with, then select AutoCorrect. Word displays the AutoCorrect dialog box and shows the symbol in the With text box. In the Replace text box, type the characters you want to use to trigger the correction, and then select Add. Word assigns the AutoCorrect entry to the symbol. Select OK to return to the Symbol dialog box and then select Close.

Inserting Symbols Using AutoCorrect

Perhaps the easiest and most efficient way to insert a symbol is via Word's AutoCorrect feature because you just need to type the two or three original characters and Word converts them to the symbol automatically. The following table lists Word's predefined AutoCorrect entries for symbols.

Type	To insert	Description
(c)	©	Copyright symbol
(r)	®	Registered trademark symbol
(tm)	™	Trademark symbol
...	. . .	Ellipsis
:(	☹	Sad emoticon
:-(	☹	Sad emoticon
:)	☺	Happy emoticon
:-)	☺	Happy emoticon
:|	☻	Indifferent emoticon
:-|	☻	Indifferent emoticon
<--	←	Thin left-pointing arrow
<==	⇐	Thick left-pointing arrow
<=>	⇔	Two-sided arrow
==>	⇒	Thick right-pointing arrow
-->	→	Thin right-pointing arrow

Setting Tabs

Documents look much better if they're properly indented and if their various parts line up nicely. The best way to do this is to use tabs instead of spaces whenever you need to create some room in a line. Why? Well, a single space can take up different amounts of room, depending on the font and size of the characters you're using. So your document can end up looking pretty ragged if you try to use spaces to indent your text. Tabs, on the other hand, are fastidiously precise: When you press the Tab key, the insertion point moves ahead exactly to the next tab stop, no more, no less.

1. Place the insertion point inside the paragraph you want to modify.

2. Select the View tab.

3. Select the Ruler check box to display the ruler.

4. Tap the ruler at the position where you want the tab to appear.

5. To move a tab, use a mouse to drag the tab left or right along the ruler.

6. To change the tab type, or to modify tabs using a touchscreen, first select the Home tab and then select the Paragraph dialog box launcher.

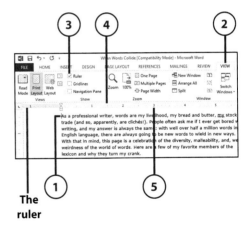

The ruler

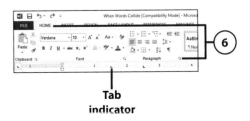

Tab indicator

7. Select Tabs to open the Tabs dialog box.

Mouse Shortcut

If you have a mouse or trackpad, a quicker way to get to the Tabs dialog box is to double-click an existing tab.

8. To change an existing tab, select it.

9. To create a new tab, type its position in the rule and then select Set.

10. Use the options in the Alignment and Leader groups to set the tab type.

11. Select OK.

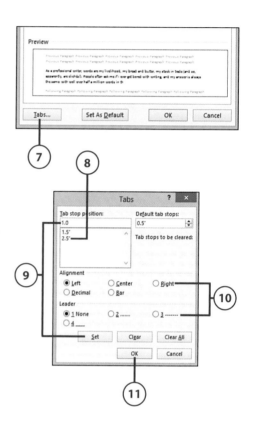

WORD'S TAB TYPES

Word has a tab to suit your every need. Here's a summary of the available types:

Left—Text lines up with the tab on the left.

Right—Text lines up with the tab on the right.

Center—Text is centered on the tab.

Decimal—Numbers line up with the tab at their decimal places.

Bar—A vertical line the height of the paragraph is added.

Leader—In this tab type, the tab space for a left, right, center, or decimal tab is filled with a bunch of characters, such as dots.

Entering Headings

Headings are special paragraphs that serve as titles for different sections of a document. You specify headings in Word by applying a heading style, where the Heading 1 style is for the main sections of the document, Heading 2 is for the subsections, Heading 3 is for the sub-subsections, and so on. In Chapter 6, "Working with Document Elements," you'll see that headings are crucial when it comes to building elements such as an outline and a table of contents.

1. Place the insertion point anywhere inside the paragraph you want to turn into a heading.

2. Select the Home tab.

3. Select the More Styles icon to open the Styles gallery.

4. Select the heading style you want to apply.

If you see the heading style you want, you can select it without opening the gallery.

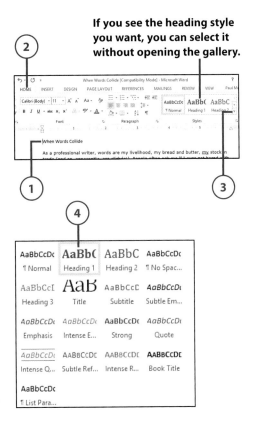

>>>Go Further

NAVIGATING WITH THE NAVIGATION PANE

Another benefit of applying headings is that you can use Word's Navigation pane to quickly and easily navigate your document. The Navigation pane has a Headings tab that displays a list of the headings in your document. When you select a heading, Word automatically jumps to that part of the file. The Navigation pane also gives you a quick view of your document's overall structure, so you can often see at a glance whether your document is correctly structured and if your headings flow smoothly and logically. To use this feature, select the View tab, select the Navigation Pane check box, and then select Headings in the Navigation pane.

Finding and Replacing Text

We're living in a world where the dream of "information at your fingertips" is fast becoming a reality. With search engines such as Google and Bing indexing online knowledge at a furious clip, and with those search engines at our beck and call full-time, thanks to wireless network connections and portable web surfing devices such as smartphones and tablets, we can call up just about any tidbit of information we need with only a minimum of fuss.

This is fine for "googleable" online info, but some of your most useful data probably resides within your own documents. Locating information in a small document is not usually a problem, but it's when your Word documents grow to tens of pages that locating the text you want becomes a real needle-in-a-haystack exercise. You can make it much easier to locate text in large documents by using Word's Find feature. Word also comes with a powerful Replace feature that enables you to quickly and easily replace multiple instances of a word or phrase with something else.

Finding Text

Word's Find feature not only locates a word or phrase, but also offers options for matching uppercase and lowercase letters, finding whole words only, and more.

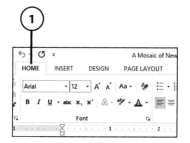

1. Select the Home tab.

2. Drop down the Find menu.

3. Select Advanced Find to open the Find and Replace dialog box.

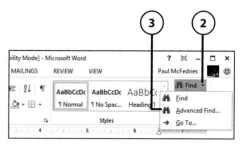

Keyboard Shortcut

You can also open the Find and Replace dialog box by pressing Ctrl+F.

---

4. Use the Find What text box to type the text you're looking for.

5. To specify search options, select More to expand the dialog box.

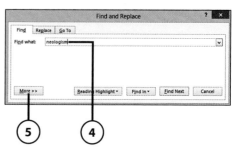

6. Select the Match Case check box to find only those instances that match the uppercase and lowercase letters you specify in the Find What text box. For example, if you type *Bob* as the search text, Find will match *Bob* but not *bob* or *BOB*.

7. Select the Find Whole Words Only check box to find only those instances of the search text that are entire words, not just partial words. For example, if you type *pen* as the search text, Find will only match the word *pen*, not words that contain pen, such as *expenses* and *pencil*.

8. Select the Use Wildcards check box to use wildcard characters in your search text. For example, you can use a question mark (?) to match any character (for example, *c?t* matches *cat*, *cut*, and *incite*, but not *colt* or *cost*) and the asterisk (*) to match any number of characters (for example, *m*t* matches *met*, *meet*, and *demerit*).

9. Select Find Next. Repeat as needed to find the instance of the text that you're looking for.

10. When you're done, select Cancel.

Word highlights the next instance of the text.

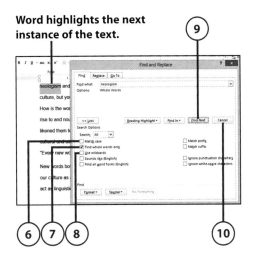

Faster Finds

For simple searches where you're just looking for a bit of text, don't bother with the Find and Replace dialog box. Instead, select the Home tab's Find icon to open the Navigation pane. Type your search term in the text box and Word automatically displays a list of the matching terms in the document.

Replacing Text

If you have a number of instances of a word or phrase that require the same edit, performing each edit manually is too time consuming. A much better method is to let Word's Replace feature handle some or all of the edits for you.

1. Select the Home tab.

2. Select Replace to open the Find and Replace dialog box with the Replace tab displayed.

Keyboard Shortcut

You can also open the Find and Replace dialog box with the Replace tab displayed by pressing Ctrl+H.

3. Type the text you want to replace in the Find What text box.

4. Type the text you want to use as the replacement in the Replace With text box.

5. If you want to specify search options, you can select More to expand the dialog box. See the section "Finding Text" for an explanation of the most important search options.

6. Select Find Next. Word highlights the next instance of the Find What text.

7. If you want to replace the highlighted text, select Replace. Word makes the replacement and then highlights the next instance. Keep

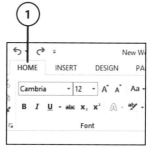

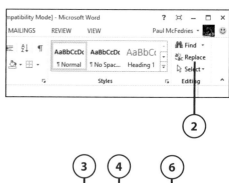

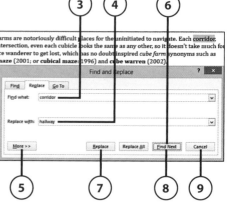

selecting this button to continue
replacing the text. Alternatively,
you can select Replace All to
replace every instance of the text
in the document.

8. If you come across an instance
    that you don't want to replace,
    select Find Next, instead.

9. When you're done, select Cancel.

REPLACING STYLES

One common Word task is to replace an existing style with another style.
For example, if you add a new main heading at the top of the document,
you might want to change all the existing Heading 1 styles to Heading 2
styles. The Replace feature makes this easy. In the Find and Replace dialog
box, select More to see the extra options. Tap inside the Find What text box,
select Format, select Style, choose the style you want to replace, and then
select OK. Tap inside the Replace With text box, select Format, select Style,
choose the style you want to use as the replacement, and then select OK.
Now run the replacement.

>>>Go Further

It's Not All Good

REPLACE ALL WITH CAUTION

The Replace All command is the quickest and easiest way to make your
replacements, but it's dangerous because you don't see every replacement
that Word makes. This is particularly true if you are using search options such
as wildcards. Unless you're absolutely certain that you want to replace every
instance in your document, use the Replace command instead of Replace All.

Proofing Text

The word *proofing* is short for *proofreading*, and it refers to inspecting a body of writing for errors or inaccuracies. No matter what kind of writing you do, always proof your work before allowing other people to read it. Why? Because one of the easiest ways to lose face in the working world or to lose marks in the academic world is to hand in a piece of writing that contains spelling or grammar mistakes. No matter how professionally organized and formatted your document appears, a simple spelling error or grammatical gaffe will stick out and take your reader's mind off your message. However, mistakes do happen, especially if your document is a large one. To help you catch these errors, Word offers both spell- and grammar-checking features.

As you type in Word, the spell checker operates in the background and examines your text for errors. When you type a word-separating character (that is, you press the spacebar or Enter or type a period, semicolon, comma, or colon), the checker compares the previous word with its internal dictionary; if it can't find the word in the dictionary, it signals a spelling error by placing a wavy red line under the word.

The grammar checker also operates in the background and scours your text for errors. When you start a new sentence, the grammar checker examines the previous sentence for problems and, if it finds any, it signals a grammatical error by placing a wavy green line under the offending word or phrase.

Checking Document Spelling and Grammar

You can handle both spelling and grammar errors as you go along, but you can also use the Spelling and Grammar task panes to gain a bit more control over the proofing tools.

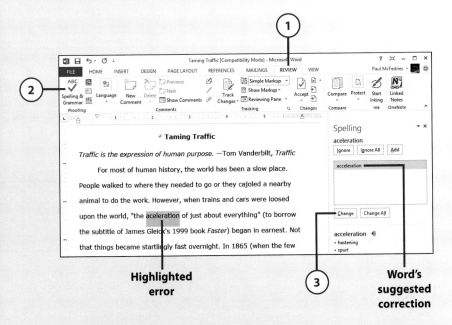

Highlighted error

Word's suggested correction

1. Select the Review tab.

2. Select Spelling & Grammar. Word displays the Spelling task pane and highlights the first error it finds.

3. Select Change. If you want to correct all instances of the error, select Change All, instead.

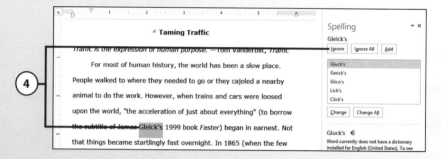

4.   If the spell checker highlights a word that you know is correct, select Ignore. If the word appears multiple times in your document, select Ignore All, instead.

Adding Correct Words to the Dictionary

Words such as proper names and technical terms are flagged by the spell checker because they don't appear in its dictionary of acceptable words. If the spell checker keeps flagging a correct word that you use frequently, you can add the word to its dictionary and thus avoid it getting flagged again. The next time the spell checker highlights the word, select Add in the Spelling task pane.

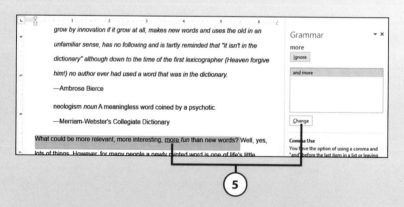

5.   If Word flags a grammatical error, you see the Grammar task pane. Select Change to apply the proposed correction. If you believe that your prose is correct, you can select Ignore, instead.

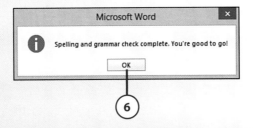

6. When the spelling and grammar check is complete, select OK.

Change the
page orientation

Set the
margins

Change the
paper size

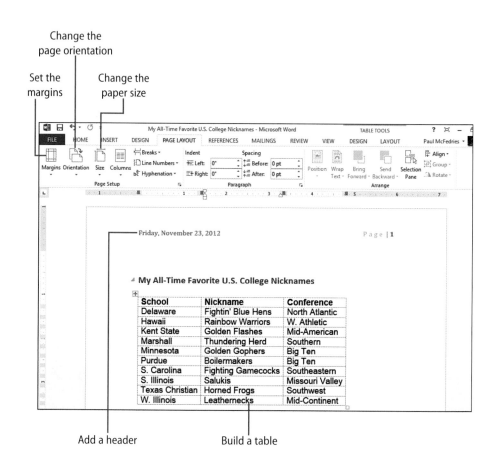

Add a header

Build a table

In this chapter, you'll learn about creating tables to hold structured data, adding headers and footers to your documents, and working with page layout options, such as margins, page orientation, and paper size.

5

→ Inserting a table into a Word document

→ Working with table rows and columns

→ Adding and populating document headers and footers

→ Setting the page margins

→ Choosing a page orientation and paper size

Working with Page Layout in Word

In the previous chapter, you dealt with Word at the "tree" level of words, sentences, and paragraphs. But getting more out of Word also requires that you deal with the program at the "forest" level of pages and documents. This means you need to get familiar with Word's page layout tools.

Page layout refers to how text and paragraphs are laid out on each page, and it involves building tables, adding headers and footers, setting margin sizes, specifying the page orientation, choosing the paper size, and so on. This chapter shows you how to work with these and other page layout features.

Building a Table

Most Word documents consist of text in the form of sentences and paragraphs. However, including lists of items in a document is common, particularly where each item in the list includes two or more details (which means a standard bulleted list won't do the job). For a short list with just a few details, the quickest way to add the list to a document is to type each item on its own line and press Tab between each detail. You could then add tab stops to the ruler (see Chapter 4, "Working with Text in Word") to line up the subitems into columns.

That works for simple items, but to construct a more complex list in the Word Web App, you can build a *table*, a rectangular structure with the following characteristics:

- Each item in the list gets its own horizontal rectangle called a *row*.

- Each set of details in the list gets its own vertical rectangle called a *column*.

- The rectangle formed by the intersection of a row and a column is called a *cell*, and you use the table cells to hold the data.

In other words, a Word table is similar to an Excel worksheet and an Access datasheet.

Inserting a Table

Although Word gives you no less than a half dozen ways to build a table, you only need to know the most straightforward method.

1. Position the insertion point where you want the table to appear.

2. Select the Insert tab.

3. Select Table.

4. Select Insert Table to display the Insert Table dialog box.

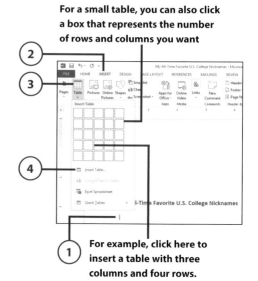

For a small table, you can also click a box that represents the number of rows and columns you want

For example, click here to insert a table with three columns and four rows.

5. Specify the number of columns you want in your table.

6. Specify the number of rows you want in the table.

7. Select OK. Word inserts the table.

8. Position the insertion point inside a cell and then add the text that you want to store in the cell. Repeat for the other cells in the table.

9. Select the Layout tab.

10. Use the Table Column Width box to set the width of the column.

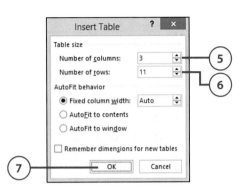

You can also set a column's width by dragging its **Move Column Width marker in the ruler.**

Displaying the Ruler

If you don't see the ruler, select the View tab and then activate the Ruler check box.

CONVERTING TEXT TO A TABLE

If you already have a list where each column is separated by a tab, comma, or some other consistent character, you can convert that list to a table. To try this out, first select the list. Select the Insert tab, then the Table command, then Convert Text to Table. Word displays the Convert Text to Table dialog box. Adjust the Number of Columns and Number of Rows values, if necessary. If you separated your columns with a character other than a tab or comma, use the Other text box to type the character. Click OK to convert the list to a table.

Selecting Table Elements

Before you can change the layout or formatting of a table, you need to select the part of the table you want to work with. Here are the techniques to use:

- **Select a cell**—Tap the cell and then select Layout, Select, Select Cell.

- **Select two or more adjacent cells**—Select one of the cells and then drag the start and end selection handles to include the other cells.

- **Select a row**—Tap any cell in the row and then select Layout, Select, Select Row.

- **Select two or more adjacent rows**—Select at least one cell in each row and then select Layout, Select, Select Row.

- **Select a column**—Tap any cell in the column and then select Layout, Select, Select Column.

- **Select two or more adjacent columns**—Select at least one cell in each column and then select Layout, Select, Select Column.

- **Select the entire table**—Tap any cell in the table and then select Layout, Select, Select Table.

Formatting a Table

To change the formatting of the table cells, you select the cells you want to work with and then use Word's standard formatting tools (font, paragraph, and so on). For more table-specific formatting, you can use the Design tab.

1. Tap inside the table.

2. Select the Design tab.

3. Select the More button of the Table Styles gallery.

If you see the style you want to apply, you can select it without opening the Table Styles gallery.

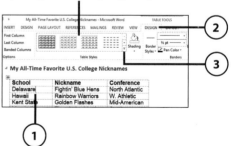

4. Select the style you want to apply to the table.

5. Select Header Row to toggle header formatting on and off for the first row. For example, in some styles the first row is given darker shading, top and bottom borders, and a bold font.

6. Select Total Row to toggle total formatting on and off for the bottom row.

7. Select Banded Rows to toggle alternating formatting for all the rows.

8. Select First Column to toggle special formatting on and off for the first column.

9. Select Last Column to toggle special formatting on and off for the last column.

10. Select Banded Columns to toggle alternating formatting for all the columns.

11. Select the cells you want to format and then use the Shading gallery to select a background color.

12. Select the cells you want to format and then use options in the Borders group to select a border style.

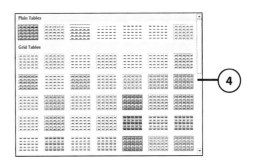

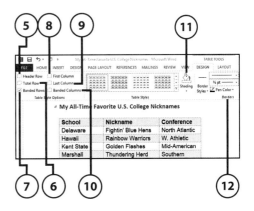

Modifying a Table Style

If the predefined table styles aren't quite what you're looking for, you can modify any style to suit your needs. Apply the style that comes closest to what you want, select the More button of the Table Styles gallery, and then select Modify Style. In the Modify Style dialog box that appears, use the controls to adjust the style's fonts, colors, borders, and more.

Adding New Rows and Columns

There are times when you need to add more data to a table. Word provides several tools that enable you to expand a table. If you're adding new items to the table, you need to add more rows; if you're adding more details to each item, you need to add more columns.

1. To add a new row at the end of the table, position the insertion point in the lower-right cell—that is, the last column of the last row—and press Tab.

2. Select the Layout tab.

3. To add a new row above an existing row, position the insertion point inside the existing row and then select Insert Above.

4. To add a new row below an existing row, position the insertion point inside the existing row and then select Insert Below.

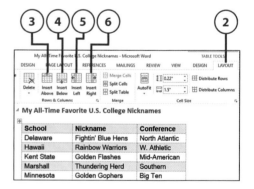

School	Nickname	Conference
Delaware	Fightin' Blue Hens	North Atlantic
Hawaii	Rainbow Warriors	W. Athletic
Kent State	Golden Flashes	Mid-American
Marshall	Thundering Herd	Southern
Minnesota	Golden Gophers	Big Ten
Purdue	Boilermakers	Big Ten
S. Carolina	Fighting Gamecocks	Southeastern
S. Illinois	Salukis	Missouri Valley
Texas Christian	Horned Frogs	Southwest
W. Illinois	Leathernecks	Mid-Continent

Adding Multiple Rows or Columns

If you want to insert multiple rows or columns, you can insert them all in one operation by first selecting the same number of existing rows or columns. For example, if you select two rows and then select Insert Below, Word inserts two rows below the selected rows.

5. To add a new column to the left of an existing column, position the insertion point inside the existing column and then select Insert Left.

6. To add a new column to the right of an existing column, position the insertion point inside the existing column and then select Insert Right.

>>>Go Further

MERGING TABLE CELLS

Although most people use tables to store lists of data, using a table to lay out a page in a particular way is also common. For example, if you are building a Word document that looks like an existing paper form or invoice, you will almost certainly need to use a table to do it. However, on most forms, not all the fields—which will be the cells in the table you create—are the same width: You might have a small field for a person's age, a much wider field for an address, and so on. Changing the row width as you learned in the previous section does not work because you need to change the sizes of individual cells.

The best way to do this is to build your table normally and then merge two or more cells together. For example, if you merge two cells that are side by side in the same row, you end up with a single cell that is twice the width of the other cells. To merge cells, first select the cells. (You can select cells in a single row, a single column, or in multiple rows and columns. However, the selection must be a rectangle of adjacent cells.) Select the Layout tab and then select Merge Cells.

Deleting Table Elements

If you find there's a part of your table you no longer need—for example, a cell, a row, or a column—you can delete it. You can delete multiple cells, rows, or columns, and, if necessary, you can also delete the entire table.

1. Select the table element you want to delete.

Selecting Elements for Deletion

If you want to delete a row or column, you need only tap anywhere inside that row or column. If you want to delete multiple rows or columns, then you need to select at least one cell in each row or column. If you plan on deleting the entire table, you need only tap anywhere inside the table.

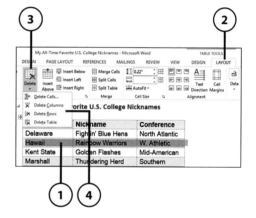

2. Select the Layout tab.

3. Select Delete.

4. Select the command that represents the type of table element you want to delete. If you select the Delete Cells command, the Delete Cells dialog box opens.

5. Select whether you want to shift the remaining cells to the left or up, or if you would rather delete the entire row or column.

6. Select OK.

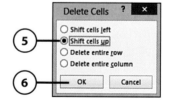

Working with Headers and Footers

A *header* is a section that appears at the top of each page between the top margin and the first line of text. Any text, graphics, or properties you insert in any header appear at the top of every page in the document. Typical header contents include the document author, the document title, and the date the document was created or modified.

A *footer* is a section that appears at the bottom of each page between the bottom margin and the last line of text. As with a header, anything you insert in any footer appears at the bottom of every page in the document. Typical footer contents include the page number and document filename.

Here are your choices for adding content to a header or footer:

- **Text**—You can type any text, such as a brief document description, a note to the reader, or your company name.

- **Page numbers**—You can insert just the page number, the phrase Page *X* (where *X* is the current page number), or Page *X* of *Y* (where *X* is the current page number and *Y* is the total number of pages in the document).

- **The current date and time**—You can display the current date, time, or both the date and time using various formats. You can also configure the date and time to update automatically each time you open the document.

- **Document information**—You can insert a number of document properties, including Author, Comments, Status, Subject, and Title.

- **A field**—Choose Design, Quick Parts, Field and then use the Field dialog box to insert the field code.

- **Picture or clip art**—You can insert a photo or other image from your computer or you can grab a piece of clip art from Office Online.

Adding a Header

You can create a header from scratch by inserting a blank header (with one or three columns) or you can select a predefined header template.

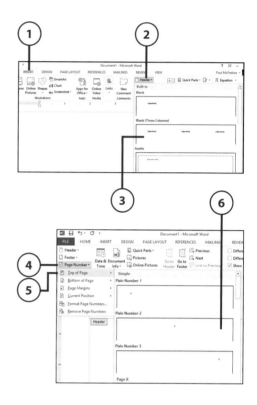

1. Select the Insert tab.

2. Select Header.

3. Select the type of header you want to add.

4. If you want to include a page number in your header, select Page Number.

5. Select Top of Page.

6. Select a page number style from the gallery.

>>>Go Further

CREATING A UNIQUE FIRST-PAGE HEADER

By default, once you define the content for one header, Word displays the same content in every header in the document. However, many situations arise in which this default behavior is not what you want. One common situation is when you want to use a different header in the first page of a document. For example, many texts use *no* header on the first page. Another example is when you want to insert document instructions or notes in the first header, but you do not want that text repeated on every page.

For these kinds of situations, you can tell Word that you want the first page's header to be different from the headers and footers in the rest of the document. You set this up by selecting the Different First Page check box. Word changes the label of the first page header to First Page Header.

7. If you want to include the date or time (or both) in your header, select Date & Time to open the Date and Time dialog box.

8. Select the format you want to use.

Updating the Date and Time Automatically

If you want Word to update the displayed date and time automatically each time you open the document, select the Update Automatically check box (in the Date and Time dialog box).

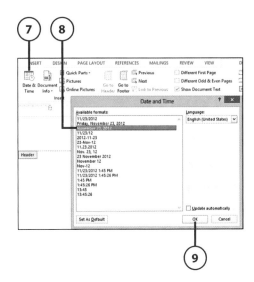

9. Select OK.

10. If you want to include a document property in your header, select Document Info.

11. Select Document Property.

12. Select the property you want to add.

13. If you want to include an image from your computer, select Pictures. See "Inserting a Picture" in Chapter 3, "Working with Office RT Graphics."

14. If you want to include clip art, select Online Pictures. See "Inserting Clip Art" in Chapter 3.

15. To add text, position the insertion point within the header and then type your text.

16. Select Close Header and Footer.

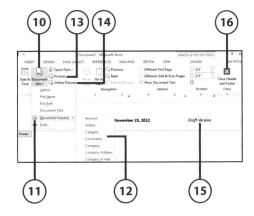

CREATING UNIQUE ODD AND EVEN PAGE HEADERS

Many documents require different layouts for the header on odd and even pages. A good example is the book you are holding. Notice that the even page header has the page number on the left and the part number and name in the middle, while the odd page header has the page number on the right and the chapter number and name in the middle.

To handle this type of situation, you can configure your document with different odd and even page headers and footers by selecting the Different Odd & Even Pages check box (on the Options drop-down list). Word changes the labels of the page headers to Even Page Header and Odd Page Header.

Adding a Footer

You can create a footer from scratch by inserting a blank footer or you can select a predefined footer template.

1. Select the Insert tab.

2. Select Footer.

3. Select the type of footer you want to add.

4. If you want to include a page number in your footer, select Page Number.

5. Select Bottom of Page.

6. Select a page number style from the gallery.

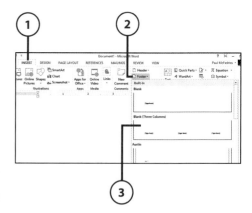

7. If you want to include the date or time (or both) in your footer, select Date & Time to open the Date and Time dialog box.

8. Select the format you want to use.

9. Select OK.

10. If you want to include a document property in your footer, select Document Info.

11. Select Document Property.

12. Select the property you want to add.

13. If you want to include an image from your computer, select Pictures. See "Inserting a Picture" in Chapter 3.

14. If you want to include clip art, select Online Pictures. See "Inserting Clip Art" in Chapter 3.

15. To add text, position the insertion point within the footer and then type your text.

16. To switch to the header, select Go to Header. Once you're in the header, you can switch back to the footer by selecting Go to Footer.

17. Select Close Header and Footer.

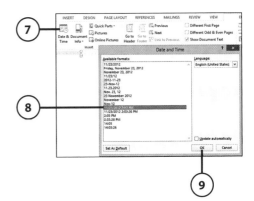

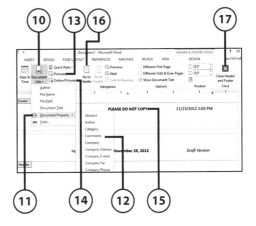

Changing the Page Setup

Word's options and features for setting up pages are legion, but few of us use them with any regularity. That's a shame because Word's page setup tools are often useful and quite easy to use, once you get to know them. The next few sections take you through the most useful of Word's page setup features.

Setting the Margins

One of the most common page layout changes is to adjust the *margins*, the blank space to the left and right, as well as above and below the document text (including the header and footer). The standard margins are one inch on all sides. Decreasing the margins fits more text on each page (which is useful when printing a long document), but it can also make the printout look cluttered and uninviting. If you increase the margins, you get less text on each page, but the added whitespace can make the document look more appealing.

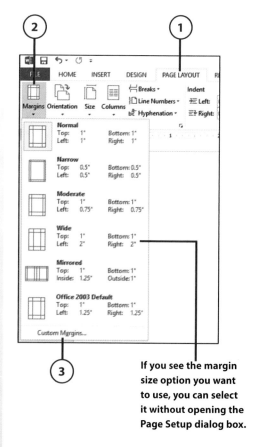

You can set specific margin sizes for the Top, Bottom, Left, and Right margins, and you can also specify where you want Word to apply the new margins: to the whole document or from the insertion point forward.

1. Select the Page Layout tab.

2. Select Margins.

3. Select Custom Margins. Word opens the Page Setup dialog box and displays the Margins tab.

If you see the margin size option you want to use, you can select it without opening the Page Setup dialog box.

4. Use the Top spin box to set the top margin.

5. Use the Bottom spin box to set the bottom margin.

6. Use the Left spin box to set the left margin.

7. Use the Right spin box to set the right margin.

Adding a Gutter

You can also set the size and position of the *gutter*, which is extra whitespace added (usually) to the inside margin to handle document binding. In the Margins tab of the Page Setup dialog box, use the Gutter spin box to set the size of the gutter, and use the Gutter Position list to select whether you want the gutter in the left margin or the top margin.

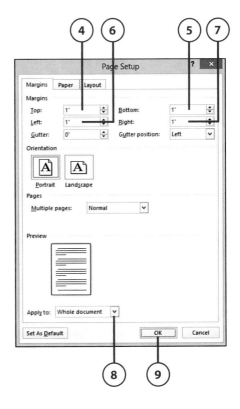

8. Use the Apply To list to select whether you want your new margins applied to the whole document or only from the insertion point forward.

9. Select OK.

Changing the Page Orientation

By default, page text runs across the short side of the page, and down the long side. This is called the *portrait orientation*. Alternatively, you can configure the text to run across the long side of the page and down the short side, which is called *landscape orientation*.

1. Select the Page Layout tab.

2. Select Orientation.

3. Select the page orientation you want to use.

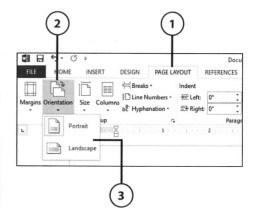

LANDSCAPE VERSUS PORTRAIT

>>>Go Further

You would use the landscape orientation mostly when you have text or an image that is too wide to fit across the page in portrait orientation. If you're using letter-size paper and your margins are set to 0.75 inches, then you have only seven inches of usable space across the page. Wide images, a table with many columns, or a long line of programming code are just a few of the situations where this width might not be enough. If you switch to landscape, however, then the usable space grows to 9.5 inches, a substantial increase.

Changing the Paper Size

Word assumes that you'll be printing your documents on standard letter-size paper, which is 8.5 inches by 11 inches. If you plan on using a different paper size, then you need to let Word know what you will be using so that it can print the document correctly.

1. Select the Page Layout tab.

2. Select Size.

3. Select More Paper Sizes. Word opens the Page Setup dialog box and displays the Paper tab.

4. Select a paper size.

5. If you need to set a custom paper width, use the Width spin box.

6. If you need to set a custom paper height, use the Height spin box.

7. Use the Apply To list to select whether you want your new paper size applied to the whole document or only from the insertion point forward.

8. Select OK.

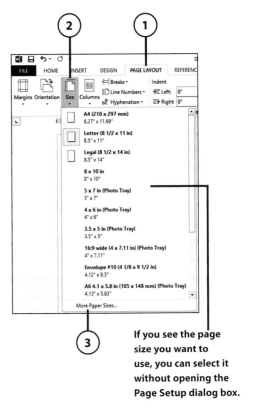

If you see the page size you want to use, you can select it without opening the Page Setup dialog box.

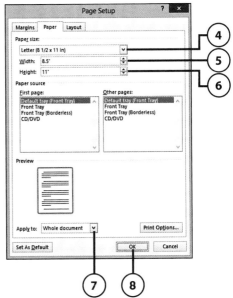

>>>Go Further

PRINTING ON THE EDGE

Getting the proper printout isn't the only reason for configuring Word to use a different page size. An old trick is to tell Word you are using a larger paper size than you actually are. Word will then print the page as if you're using the larger size, which with some experimentation means you can get Word to print right to (or pretty close to) the edge of a regular sheet of paper or an envelope.

Create a table
of contents

Insert footnotes
and endnotes

Mark index entries
and create an index

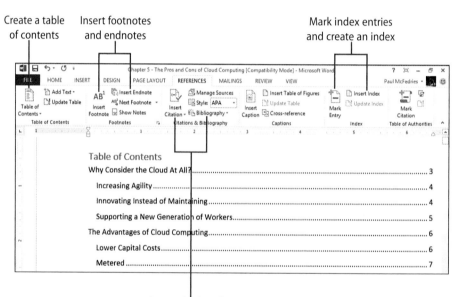

Insert citations for
a bibliography

In this chapter, you'll learn a number of techniques for taking your Word documents to the next level, including outlines, footnotes, and indexes.

→ Using an outline to keep your document organized
→ Augmenting a document with footnotes and endnotes
→ Building a bibliography for a document's sources
→ Creating a table of contents
→ Generating an index of the words and phrases in a document

Working with Document Elements

If you want to take your documents to a higher level, Word certainly has powerful tools that can help you get there. However, as any carpenter or cook will tell you, powerful tools alone are not enough to ensure a good result. You have to know how to wield those tools, of course, but you also need to know *why* you want to use those tools. In other words, when you use a tool, you should have some sort of objective in mind.

One very useful objective is to ensure your document presents its information in a manner that is both logical and consistent. Another laudable goal is to create a document that has high-quality, trustworthy information. A third goal is a document that provides features that make it easy for the reader to see at a glance what's in the document and to find specific information in the document.

The Word features you'll learn about in this chapter can help you realize all of these goals (and many others). An outline helps you build a document with a logical, consistent structure. The judicious use of footnotes and endnotes, and the addition of a comprehensive bibliography ensure others see your information as trustworthy. And inserting a table of contents and a high-quality index can help readers see what's in your document and find the information they need.

Keeping a Document Organized Using an Outline

Most documents have titles, headings, and subheadings that determine the underlying organizational structure of the document. An outline is simply a summary of this structure that lets you see, at a glance, how the document is set up. If things don't look right, you can then use the outline structure to easily reorganize the document.

Note that in Word you do not "create" an outline. Instead, the outline builds itself naturally out of the document's Heading styles—Heading 1 through Heading 9—which correspond to level numbers in the outline: Heading 1 is Level 1, Heading 2 is Level 2, and so on.

Organizing Your Document with an Outline

You will most often use an outline to get an overall view of your document structure, but you can also use an outline to expand and collapse outline levels, promote and demote items to different levels, and rearrange elements of your document.

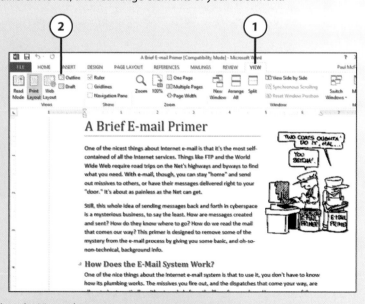

1. Select the View tab.
2. Select Outline. Word switches the document to Outline view.

Word displays nonheading paragraphs with a bullet.

Word displays the Outlining tab.

Word hides elements such as graphics and headers.

Word displays a plus sign (+) icon beside each paragraph formatted with a Heading style.

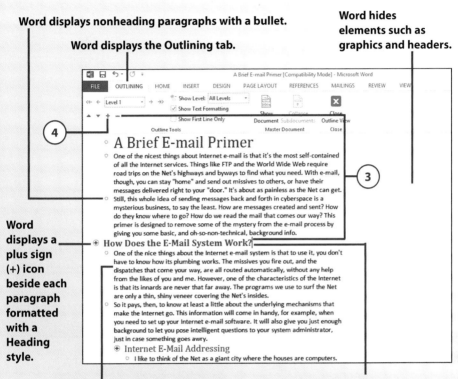

Word displays lower-level headings indented from the left margin.

Word displays Heading 1 paragraphs flush with the left margin.

3. To collapse an outline level, position the insertion point inside the level and then select Collapse. The first time you run the Collapse command, Word hides all the body text within the level, including the body text of all the item's subheadings. Each subsequent time you run the Collapse command, Word hides the lowest level within the item.

Keyboard Shortcut

You can also collapse an outline level by pressing Alt+Shift+_.

4. To expand an outline level, position the insertion point inside the level and then select Expand. Word expands the item's subheadings and body text in the opposite order that it collapses them.

Keyboard Shortcut

You can also expand an outline level by pressing Alt+Shift++.

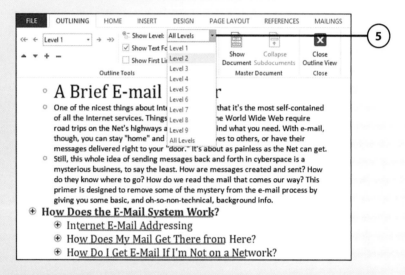

5. To set the number of outline levels that Word displays, use the Show Level list to select the lowest level that you want to view.

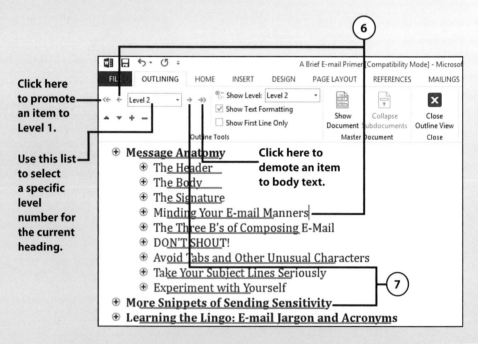

Click here to promote an item to Level 1.

Use this list to select a specific level number for the current heading.

Click here to demote an item to body text.

6. To *promote* an outline level (that is, move the item to a higher level), position the insertion point inside the level and then select Promote.

Keyboard Shortcut

You can also promote an outline level by pressing Alt+Shift+Left arrow.

7. To *demote* an outline level (that is, move the item to a lower level), position the insertion point inside the level and then select Demote.

Keyboard Shortcut

You can also demote an outline level by pressing Alt+Shift+Right arrow.

8. To move an item up within the outline, position the insertion point inside the item and then select Move Up.

Keyboard Shortcut

You can also move an item up in the outline by pressing Alt+Shift+Up arrow.

9. To move an item down within the outline, position the insertion point inside the item and then select Move Down.

Keyboard Shortcut

You can also move an item down in the outline by pressing Alt+Shift+Down arrow.

10.   When you're finished with the outline, select Close Outline View.

DEFINING OUTLINE LEVELS FOR CUSTOM STYLES

Word's default outlines are based on the Heading 1 through Heading 9 styles, which correspond to outline levels 1 through 9. However, what if your documents don't use the Heading styles? For example, you may have to follow corporate style guidelines and templates that dictate other styles for titles, subtitles, headings, and subheadings.

In this case, you can still use the Outline view, but first you must modify your custom heading styles to assign each one the corresponding outline level. In Word's Home tab, click the dialog box launcher in the lower-right corner of the Styles group to open the Styles pane. Tap and hold (or right-click) the style you want to work with and then select Modify to open the Modify Style dialog box. Select Format, then Paragraph to display the Paragraph dialog box, use the Outline Level list to select the outline level you want to associate with the style, and then select OK. Repeat as needed for each of the other heading styles you want to assign an outline level.

Adding Footnotes and Endnotes

A *footnote* is a short note at the bottom of a page that provides extra information about something mentioned in the regular text on that page. Word indicates a footnote with a *reference mark*, a number or other symbol that appears as a superscript in both the regular text and in a special footnote box at the bottom of the page. You can also place all of your footnotes at the end of the document, in which case they are called *endnotes*.

Word makes working with footnotes and endnotes a breeze. Not only are they easy to insert, but Word also keeps track of the reference marks and updates the numbers (or whatever) automatically no matter where you insert new notes in the document.

Inserting a Footnote or Endnote

A default footnote appears at the bottom of the current page and uses Arabic numerals (1, 2, 3, and so on) as the reference marks. A default endnote appears at the end of the document and uses lowercase Roman numerals (i, ii, iii, and so on) as the reference marks.

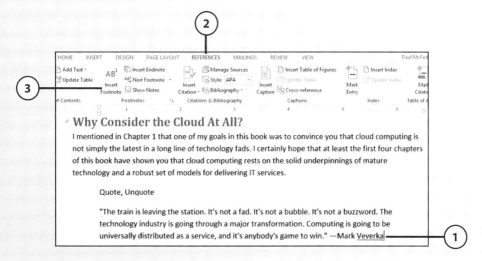

1. Position the insertion where you want the footnote or endnote reference mark to appear.

2. Select the References tab.

3. Select Insert Footnote. If you prefer to insert an endnote, select the Insert Endnote command, instead.

Keyboard Shortcut

You can also insert a footnote by pressing Ctrl+Alt+F. If you want to insert an endnote, instead, press Ctrl+Alt+D.

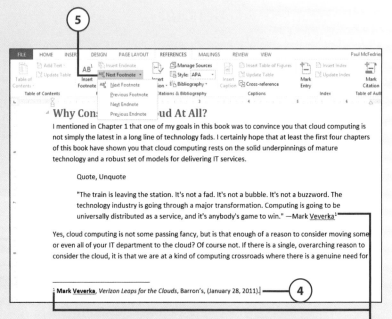

Word inserts the reference mark in the text and in the note area.

4. Type your note text.

5. To navigate footnotes or endnotes, select Next Footnote and then select whether you want to see the next or previous footnote or endnote.

>>>GoFurther

CREATING CUSTOM FOOTNOTES AND ENDNOTES

If Word's default footnotes and endnotes are not what you need, the program has plenty of options you can wield to customize your notes. For example, you can position the footnote area below the last line of the page instead of at the bottom of the page; for the reference marks, you can use Arabic numerals, uppercase or lowercase letters, uppercase or lowercase Roman numerals, or symbols such as the following: *, †, ‡, §. In fact, you can use any symbol available in the Symbol dialog box; you can start the reference marks at a specific number, letter, or symbol; and you can have the reference marks restart with each page or each section.

To create a custom footnote or endnote that uses some or all of these options, position the insertion point where you want the reference mark to appear, select the References tab, and then select the dialog box launcher in the lower-right corner of the Footnotes tab. Word displays the Footnote and Endnote dialog box. Select your options and then select Insert.

Inserting Citations and a Bibliography

In a scholarly document, if you reference someone else's results, ideas, or work, you must provide a citation for that reference so that other people can see the original work for themselves. The documentation style of the citation depends on the citation guidelines that your company, publisher, or teacher uses. The most popular documentation styles come from the Modern Language Association (MLA), *The Chicago Manual of Style* (Chicago), and the American Psychological Association (APA).

Word offers comprehensive tools for inserting citations, working with citation styles, creating and managing sources, and inserting bibliographies based on your document's sources. The next few sections take you through the details.

Inserting Citations and a Bibliography

To create a bibliography in Word, you first add citations each time you reference another person's work in your document, and you then gather those citations into your bibliography.

1. Position the insertion point where you want the citation to appear.

2. Select the References tab.

3. Use the Style list to select the citation style you prefer.

4. Select Insert Citation.

5. Select Add New Source. Word displays the Create Source dialog box.

6. Use the Type of Source list to select the type of source material you used.

7. Type the bibliographic data in the text boxes provided, which vary depending on the type of source you chose.

8. Select OK to insert the citation. Repeat steps 4 through 8 to insert your other citations.

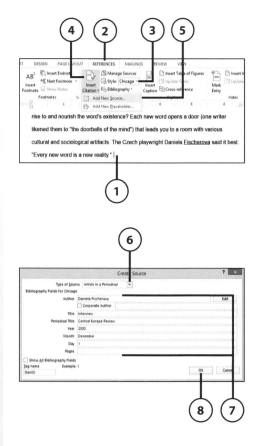

9. Position the insertion point where you want the bibliography to appear.

10. Select the References tab.

11. Use the Style list to select the bibliography style you prefer.

12. Select Bibliography.

13. Select Insert Bibliography. Word inserts the bibliography.

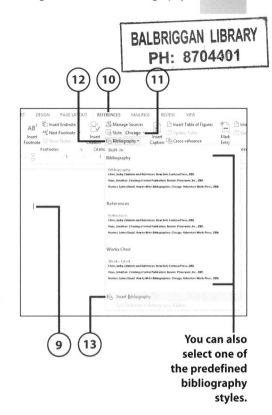

You can also select one of the predefined bibliography styles.

Updating Your Bibliography

If you add, edit, or delete sources in your document, be sure to update your bibliography. Tap and hold (or right-click) the bibliography and then click Update Field. Note, too, that you can change the bibliography's documentation style by tapping or clicking the bibliography, selecting the References tab, and then using the Style list to select the style you want to use.

MANAGING YOUR SOURCES

>>>Go Further

Word maintains a list of sources in the current document as well as a master list of sources that you've added in all documents. You can use the Source Manager feature to copy sources from the master list to the current document, which makes it easy to reuse sources in different documents. Source Manager also enables you to edit and delete sources and perform searches for the source you need.

To work with Source Manager, select the References tab and then select Manage Sources. The Master List is the list of sources you've added to all your documents, while the Current List is the list of sources added to the current document. Sources with check marks beside them have been used in citations. Use the Copy, Delete, Edit, and New button to work with your sources.

Inserting a Table of Contents

As a book reader, you need no introduction to the idea of a table of contents (TOC). In fact, if you're like most savvy computer book buyers, you probably take a good long look at a book's TOC before deciding whether to purchase it. However, you may not be as familiar with TOCs as they apply to Word documents. That's not surprising if you normally deal only with documents that are just a few pages long. However, when a document gets to be 5 or 10 pages long with multiple headings and subheadings, putting a TOC at or near the beginning of the document is a good idea for the following reasons:

- The TOC gives the reader a good sense of the overall structure of the document.
- You can include page numbers in the TOC, which enables the reader of a document printout to easily find a particular section.
- You can set up the TOC entries as hyperlinks to the corresponding sections within the document, so your readers are always just a Ctrl+click away from any section.

Like the items you see in Outline view, Word also generates the entries that make up a TOC from a document's Heading styles. This concept makes sense because a TOC is, by definition, a listing of the main headings in a document, as they appear within that document.

Adding a Table of Contents to a Document

Word offers several predefined TOC styles, but you can also use Word's TOC options to create a custom table of contents.

1. Position the insertion point where you want the TOC to appear.

2. Select the References tab.

3. Select Table of Contents.

4. Select Custom Table of Contents. Word displays the Table of Contents dialog box.

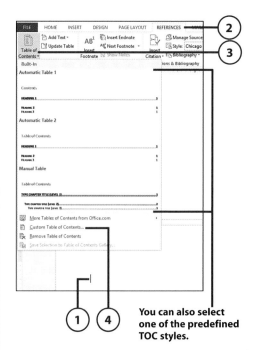

You can also select one of the predefined TOC styles.

5. If you want to base your TOC on a template, use the Formats list to select the template you want to start off with.

6. Select the Show Page Numbers check box to toggle page numbers on and off in the TOC.

7. If you are showing page numbers in your TOC, select the Right Align Page Numbers check box to toggle the right alignment of the page numbers on and off.

8. If you are showing right-aligned page numbers in your TOC, use the Tab Leader list to select the leader you want to appear between the headings and the page numbers.

9. Select the Use Hyperlinks Instead of Page Numbers check box to toggle hyperlinks on and off.

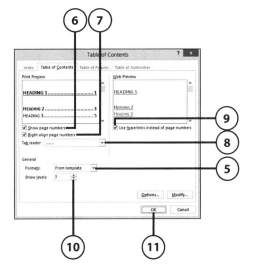

Hyperlinks and Page Numbers

The Use Hyperlinks Instead of Page Numbers check box is poorly named. If you activate this option, Word still uses page numbers in Page Layout, Outline, and Draft views, but it does not display page numbers in the Web Layout and Full Screen Reading views. In all views, the headings are formatted as hyperlinks.

10. Use the Show Levels spin box to click the number of heading levels you want in the TOC.

11. Select OK. Word inserts the TOC.

Updating a TOC

If you add, remove, or edit your document headings, or if you add content that causes the page numbers to change, be sure to update your TOC. Select the References tab and then select Update Table. In the Update Table of Contents dialog box, select the Update Page Numbers Only option if your document headings haven't changed; select the Update Entire Table option, instead, if your headings have changed.

Generating an Index

I mentioned earlier that one of the first things a savvy computer book buyer (that's you) does before making a decision on a book is to give the book's TOC a good going-over. In many cases, the second thing is giving the book's index a good look, too. Even if you don't check out the index *before* buying a book, there's a good chance you make regular use of the index *after* buying it. In almost all nonfiction books, a good index is an essential feature.

Is it essential in your Word documents? That depends on several factors:

- **Length**—The longer the document, the more likely an index is necessary or expected.

- **Complexity**—The more complex a document's subject matter, the more likely an index helps cut through that complexity and enables your readers to find what they want.

- **Audience**—Some people simply *expect* an index and are inordinately upset if a document does not include one.

If you have a document that has some or all of these factors, then you ought to consider adding an index. However, I should mention early on that creating an index is tedious, time-consuming, and finicky work. Although some techniques are available that you can use to lighten the load, you should not make the decision to include an index lightly. Finally, although building a quality index for a large document such as a book requires special training, Word's indexing tools are all you really need for more modest projects.

Marking Entries and Creating an Index

You generate an index by first marking the various instances of text in your document that you want to use as index entries. Once that's done, Word can build the index automatically from these marked entries.

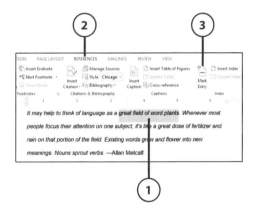

1. Select the text you want to use as an index entry.

2. Select the References tab.

3. Select Mark Entry. Word displays the Mark Index Entry dialog box.

Keyboard Shortcut

You can also run the Mark Entry command by pressing Alt+Shift+X.

---

4. The text you select appears in the Main entry text box, but if you want this text to be a subentry instead, cut the text and paste it in the Subentry text box.

5. Type the Main Entry text.

6. If you want the reader to refer to a different index entry, select Cross-reference and then type the entry name.

7. If the index entry is important in some way, select Bold and/or

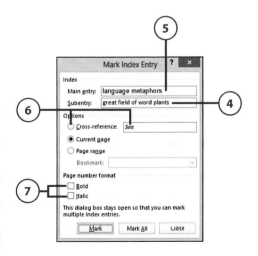

Italic. For example, these formats are often used to highlight entries that define the concept or that discuss the concept in a major way.

8. Click Mark. If the selected text appears in multiple places in the document, click Mark All. Word leaves the dialog box open for more entries, so repeat steps 1 to 7 to mark other entries in the document.

9. Select Close.

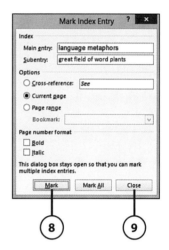

Hiding the Formatting Marks

After you mark your first index entry, Word turns on its formatting marks so you can see the otherwise hidden index fields. To hide these marks, select the Home tab and then select Show/Hide ¶ (or press Ctrl+*).

10. Position the insertion point where you want the index to appear.

11. Select the References tab.

12. Select Insert Index. Word displays the Index dialog box.

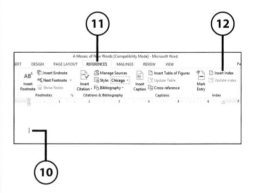

13. If you want to base your custom index on a template, use the Formats list to select the template you want to start off with.

14. Select the Right Align Page Numbers check box to toggle the right alignment of the page numbers on and off.

15. If you are right-aligning your page numbers, use the Tab Leader list to select the leader you want to appear between the entries and the page numbers.

16. Select Indented to show the subentries on separate lines. Select Run-in, instead, to show each group of the subentries in a single paragraph. (Clicking Run-in disables the Right Align Page Numbers check box.)

17. Click OK. Word inserts the index.

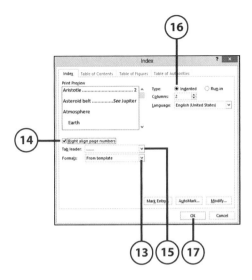

>>>Go Further

MARKING ENTRIES WITH A CONCORDANCE FILE

The process of selecting each entry in the document can really slow you down. If you have a good idea of the words and phrases you want to include in your index, you can set up a separate *concordance file*, a Word document that includes these words and phrases, either as main entries or as subentries. You can then use Word's AutoMark feature to mark all the concordance items as index entries.

The concordance file is a regular Word document that contains a two-column table, where you use the left column to type the word or phrase that you want Word to look for in the document you are indexing, and you use the right column to type the word or phrase that you want Word to use as the index entry. If you want to create both a main entry and a subentry, separate them with a colon.

With the concordance file completed and saved, switch to the document you want to index, select the References tab, and then select Insert Index to display the Index dialog box. Select AutoMark to display the Open Index AutoMark File dialog box, select the concordance file, and then select Open. Word marks all the concordance items as index entries.

Create formulas   Add functions to formulas

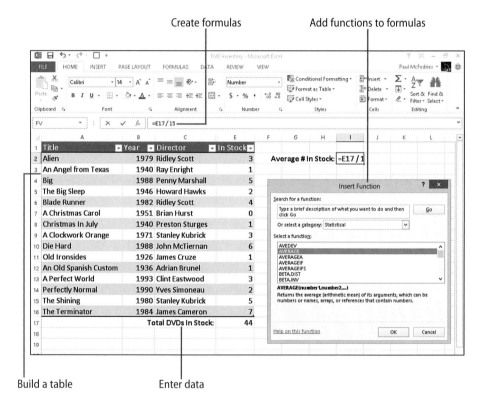

Build a table   Enter data

In this chapter, you'll learn about entering data into an Excel worksheet, building formulas, working with functions, and storing data in tables.

→ Entering numbers, text, dates, and times
→ Editing cell data
→ Building formulas to add calculations to a worksheet
→ Creating and working with Excel tables

Entering Excel Data

If you've never used a spreadsheet before, Excel may seem intimidating and getting it to do anything useful may seem like a daunting task. However, a spreadsheet is really just a fancy electronic version of a numeric scratch pad. With the latter, you write down a few numbers and then use elementary school techniques to calculate a result. At its most basic level, an Excel worksheet is much the same: You type one or more values and then you create a formula that calculates a result.

The first part of this basic Excel method is entering your worksheet data, and that's what this chapter is all about. You learn the best ways to get your data into the worksheet, some tips and tricks for easier data entry, how to build formulas, and how to use tables to make your data easier to read and understand.

Understanding Worksheet Cells and Data

A worksheet is a rectangular arrangement of rows and columns. The rows are numbered, where the topmost row is 1, the row below it is 2, and so on all the way to 1,048,576. (Although, as you can imagine, worksheets that use more than a million rows are quite rare!) The columns are labeled with letters, where A is the leftmost column, the next column is B, and so on. After column Z come columns AA, AB, and so on, all the way up to XFD; that's 16,384 columns in all.

The intersection of each row and column is called a *cell*, and each cell has a unique address that combines its column letter (or letters) and row number. For example, the upper-left cell in a worksheet is at the intersection of column A and row 1, so its address is A1. When you click a cell, it becomes the *active cell*—which Excel designates by surrounding the cell with a heavy border and by displaying a small square in the lower-right corner—and its address appears in the Name box, which is located just above column A.

You use these worksheet cells to enter your data, which you learn more about in the next few sections. For now, you should know that worksheet cells can hold four kinds of data:

- **Numbers**—These entries can be dollar values, weights, interest rates, or any other numerical quantity.

- **Text**—These entries are usually labels such as *August Sales* or *Territory* that make a worksheet easier to read, but they can also be text/number combinations for items such as phone numbers and account codes.

- **Dates and times**—These entries are specific dates (such as 8/23/2013), specific times (such as 9:05 a.m.), or combinations of the two. You mostly use dates (and, to a lesser extent, times) in tables and lists to record when something took place, although Excel also lets you calculate with dates and times.

- **Formulas**—These are calculations involving two or more values, such as 2*5 or A1+A2+A3. See the "Working with Formulas and Functions" section later in this chapter.

Working with Numbers

Worksheets are all about numbers. You add them together, subtract them, take their average, or perform any number of mathematical operations on them. Excel recognizes that you're entering a number if you start the entry with a decimal point (.), a plus sign (+), a minus sign (-), or a dollar sign ($). Here are some other rules for entering numbers:

- You can enter percentages by following the number with a percent sign (%). Excel stores the number as a decimal. For example, the entry **15%** is stored as 0.15.

- You can use scientific notation when entering numbers. For example, to enter the number 3,879,000,000, you could enter **3.879E+09**.

- You can also use parentheses to indicate a negative number. If you make an entry such as **(125)**, Excel assumes you mean negative 125.

- You can enter commas to separate thousands, but you have to make sure that each comma appears in the appropriate place. Excel will interpret an entry such as **12,34** as text.

- If you want to enter a fraction, you need to type an integer, a space, and then the fraction (**5 1/8**, for example). This is true even if you're entering only the fractional part; in this case, you need to type a zero, a space, and then the fraction or else Excel will interpret the entry as a date. For example, **0 1/8** is the fraction one eighth, but **1/8** is January 8.

Working with Text

In Excel, text entries can include any combination of letters, symbols, and numbers. Although text is sometimes used as data, you'll find that you mostly use text to describe the contents of your worksheets. This is very important because even a modest-sized spreadsheet can become a confusing jumble of numbers without some kind of guideline to keep things straight. There is no practical limit on the length of text entries (they can be up to 32,767 characters long!), but in general, you shouldn't use anything too fancy or elaborate; a simple phrase such as *Monthly Expenses* or *Payment Date* will usually suffice.

Working with Dates and Times

Excel uses *serial numbers* to represent specific dates and times. To get a date serial number, Excel uses December 31, 1899, as an arbitrary starting point and counts the number of days that have passed since then. For example, the date serial number for January 1, 1900, is 1; for January 2, 1900, it is 2; and so on. Table 7.1 displays some examples of date serial numbers.

Table 7.1   Examples of Date Serial Numbers

Serial Number	Date
366	December 31, 1900
16229	June 6, 1944
41639	December 31, 2013

To get a time serial number, Excel expresses time as a decimal fraction of the 24-hour day to get a number between 0 and 1. The starting point, midnight, is given the value 0, so noon—halfway through the day—has a serial number of 0.5. Table 7.2 displays some examples of time serial numbers.

Table 7.2   Examples of Time Serial Numbers

Serial Number	Time
0.25	6:00:00 AM
0.375	9:00:00 AM
0.70833	5:00:00 PM
.99999	11:59:59 PM

You can combine the two types of serial numbers. For example, 41639.5 represents noon on December 31, 2013.

The advantage of using serial numbers in this way is that it makes calculations involving dates and times very easy. A date or time is really just a number, so any mathematical operation you can perform on a number you can also perform on a date. This is invaluable for worksheets that track delivery times, monitor accounts receivable or accounts payable aging, calculate invoice discount dates, and so on.

Although it's true that the serial numbers make it easier for the computer to manipulate dates and times, it's not the best format for humans to comprehend. For example, the number 25,404.95555 is meaningless, but the moment it represents (July 20, 1969, at 10:56 PM EDT) is one of the great moments in history (the *Apollo 11* moon landing). Fortunately, Excel takes care of the conversion between these formats so that you never have to worry about it.

To enter a date or time, use any of the formats outlined in Table 7.3.

Table 7.3   Excel Date and Time Formats

Format	Example
m/d	8/23
m/d/yy	8/23/13
d-mmm	23-Aug (Excel assumes the current year)
d-mmm-yy	23-Aug-13
mmm-yy	Aug-13 (Excel assumes the first day of the month)
mmmm-yy	August-13
mmmm d, yyyy	August 23, 2013
dddd, mmmm d, yyyy	Monday, August 23, 2013
h:mm AM/PM	3:10 PM
h:mm:ss AM/PM	3:10:45 PM
h:mm	15:10
h:mm:ss	15:10:45
mm:ss.0	10:45.7
m/d/yy h:mm AM/PM	8/23/13 3:10 PM
m/d/yy h:mm	8/23/13 15:10

Entering and Editing Data

A spreadsheet is only as useful—and as accurate—as the data it contains. Even a small mistake can render your results meaningless. So the first rule of good spreadsheet style is to enter and edit your data carefully.

Entering Cell Data

If you're new to spreadsheet work, you'll no doubt be pleased to hear that entering data into a worksheet cell is straightforward.

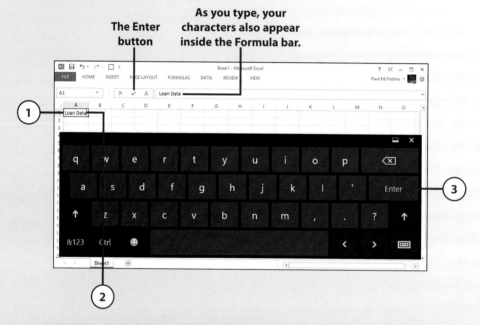

The Enter button

As you type, your characters also appear inside the Formula bar.

1. Select the cell you want to use to enter your data. The easiest way to do this is to tap the cell, but you can also use the arrow keys to navigate to the cell you want.

2. Type your data. Excel automatically opens the cell for editing and places your typing inside the cell.

3. When your entry is complete, press Enter. Excel moves the active cell to the cell below. If you don't want the active cell to move after you confirm your entry, tap the Enter button, instead.

Confirming Data Entry with the Arrow Keys

You can also confirm your entry by pressing any of the arrow keys or by tapping another cell. The active cell moves either in the direction of the arrow or to the cell you tapped. This feature is handy if you have, say, a lengthy row of data to type in. By pressing (in this case) the right arrow key to confirm each entry, you automatically move the active cell along the row.

Editing Cell Data

If you make a mistake when entering data or you have to update the contents of a cell, you need to edit the cell to get the correct value. If you want to replace the entire cell contents, follow the steps in the previous section. This section shows you how to make changes to a cell's existing content.

Insertion point

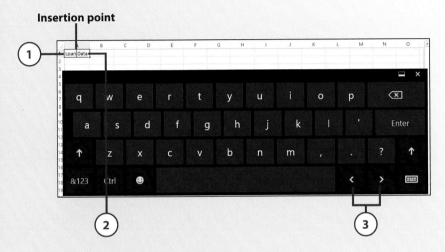

1. Select the cell you want to edit.
2. Double-tap the cell. The insertion point appears inside the cell at the end of the entry.

Keyboard Shortcut
You can also open the active cell for editing by pressing F2.

3. Use the left and right arrow keys to position the insertion point where you want to make your changes.

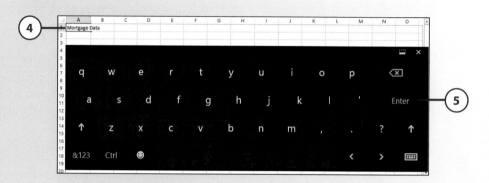

4. Edit the contents of the cell.

5. Confirm your changes by pressing Enter. To cancel the edit without confirming your changes, press Esc.

Working with Formulas and Functions

Any worksheet is merely a collection of numbers and text until you define some kind of relationship between the various entries. You do this by creating *formulas* that perform calculations and produce results. This section takes you through some formula basics and then shows you how to build your own formulas.

Excel divides formulas into three main groups: arithmetic, comparison, and text. Each group has its own set of operators, and you use each group in different ways.

Let's start with *arithmetic formulas*, which are by far the most common type of formula. They combine numbers, cell addresses, and function results with mathematic operators to perform calculations. Table 7.4 summarizes the mathematic operators used in arithmetic formulas.

Table 7.4   The Arithmetic Operators

Operator	Name	Example	Result
+	Addition	=10+5	15
-	Subtraction	=10-5	5
-	Negation	=-10	-10
*	Multiplication	=10*5	50

Operator	Name	Example	Result
/	Division	=10/5	2
%	Percentage	=10%	.1
^	Exponentiation	=10^5	100,000

Most of the operators in Table 7.4 are straightforward, but the exponentiation operator may require further explanation. The formula $=x^\wedge y$ means that the value x is raised to the power y. For example, $=3^\wedge 2$ produces the result 9 (that is, 3*3=9). Similarly, $=2^\wedge 4$ produces 16 (that is, 2*2*2*2=16).

A *comparison formula* is a statement that compares two or more numbers, text strings, cell contents, or function results. If the statement is true, the result of the formula is given the logical value TRUE (which is equivalent to 1). If the statement is false, the formula returns the logical value FALSE (which is equivalent to 0). Table 7.5 summarizes the operators you can use in comparison formulas.

Table 7.5   Comparison Formula Operators

Operator	Name	Example	Result
=	Equal to	=10=5	FALSE
>	Greater than	=10>5	TRUE
<	Less than	=10<5	FALSE
>=	Greater than or equal to	="a">="b"	FALSE
<=	Less than or equal to	="a"<="b"	TRUE
<>	Not equal to	="a"<>"b"	TRUE

There are many uses for comparison formulas. For example, you could determine whether to pay a salesperson a bonus by using a comparison formula to compare the person's actual sales with a predetermined quota. If the sales are greater than the quota, the salesperson is awarded the bonus. Another example is credit collection. If the amount a customer owes is, say, over 150 days past due, then you might send the receivable to a collection agency.

Building a Formula

Building a formula is very much like entering data into a cell, with the exception that all Excel formulas must begin with an equal sign (=).

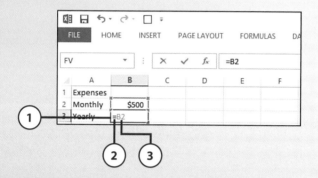

1. Select the cell you want to use for the formula.

2. Type an equal sign (=). Excel opens the cell for editing and enters the equal sign.

3. Enter a value, cell reference, range, range name, or function name.

Tapping to Enter a Cell Address

When entering a cell reference in a formula, you could just type in the cell address, but it's often faster and more accurate to let Excel do the work by tapping the cell. The address appears automatically in the formula at the insertion point.

4. Enter an operator (such as + or *).

5. Repeat steps 3 and 4 until the formula is complete.

6. Press Enter to accept the formula.

CONTROLLING THE ORDER OF CALCULATION

When you use the operators listed earlier in Tables 7.4 and 7.5, be aware that Excel processes the operators not only from left to right, but also by giving some operators precedence over others. For example, Excel always performs multiplication and division before it performs addition and subtraction. In some cases, you might need to control the order of calculation so that, say, Excel performs an addition operation before it performs a multiplication. To do this, enclose the operation you want performed first in parentheses. Excel always calculates expressions enclosed in parentheses first, so you can use this technique to force Excel to calculate your formulas in whatever order you require.

Understanding Functions

Consider the following scenario: You want to deposit a certain amount in an investment that earns a particular rate of interest over a particular number of years. Assuming you start at 0, how much will the investment be worth at the end of the term? Given a present value (represented by *pv*), a regular payment (*pmt*), an annual interest rate (*rate*), and some number of years (*nper*), here's the formula that calculates the future value of the investment:

```
pv(1 + rate) ^ nper + pmt * (((1 + rate) ^ nper) - 1) / rate
```

That's a *really* complex formula, but this complexity wouldn't be a big deal if this formula were obscure or rarely used. However, calculating the future value of an investment is one of the most common Excel chores (it is, for example, the central calculation in most retirement planning models). Having to type such a formula once is bad enough, but it is one you may need dozens of times. Clearly, entering such a formula by hand so many times is both extremely time consuming and prone to errors.

Fortunately, Excel offers a solution: a worksheet function called FV(), which reduces the earlier formula to the following:

```
fv(rate, nper, pmt, pv)
```

Not only is this formula much simpler to use and faster to type, you also don't have to memorize anything other than the function name because, as you'll soon see, Excel shows you the full function syntax (that is, the list of arguments and the order in which they appear) as you type it.

In general, a *function* is a predefined formula that calculates a result based on one or more *arguments*, which are the function's input values (such as `rate` and `nper` in the FV() example). Note that most functions have at least one argument, and that for functions with two or more arguments, in most cases some of those arguments are required (that is, Excel returns an error if the arguments are not present) and some are optional.

Functions not only simplify complex mathematical formulas, but they also enable you to perform powerful calculations such as statistical correlation, the number of workdays between two dates, and square roots.

Adding a Function Directly to a Cell

The quickest way to include a function in a formula is to type the function and its arguments directly into the cell.

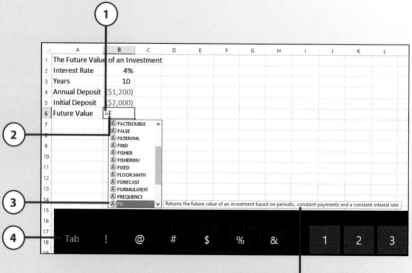

Excel displays a description
of the selected function.

1. Enter your formula up to the point where you want to include the function.

2. Begin typing the function name. As you type, Excel displays a list of function names that begin with what you have typed so far.

3. Tap a function name to select it and see its description.

4. To add the selected function name to the formula, press Tab. Excel adds the function name and a left parenthesis: (.

Excel displays the function's syntax.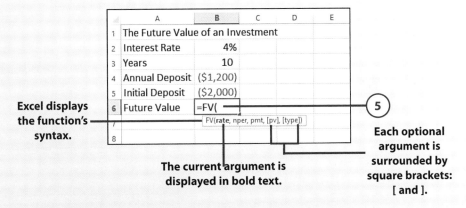

The current argument is displayed in bold text.

Each optional argument is surrounded by square brackets: [and].

5. If you're typing the function name by hand, be sure to add the left parenthesis after the name. Excel now displays a ScreenTip with the function syntax.

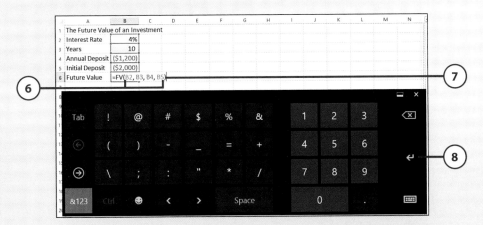

6. Enter the required arguments, separated by commas. If you also need to use any of the optional arguments, enter them separated by commas.

7. Type the right parenthesis:).

8. Press Enter. Excel enters the formula and displays the formula result in the cell.

Adding a Function Using the Function Wizard

Excel's pop-up function list and syntax screen tips are so useful that typing functions by hand is almost always the fastest way to incorporate functions into your formulas. However, if you're not sure which function you need, or if you want to see the function results before committing the function to the formula, then you need to turn to Excel's Function Wizard.

1. Enter your formula up to the point where you want to include the function.

2. Select the Formulas tab.

3. Select Insert Function. You can also click the Insert Function button beside the Formula bar. The Insert Function dialog box opens.

The Most Recently Used List

Excel maintains a list of the last 10 functions you have used. If the function you want is one that you used recently, click Most Recently Used in the list of categories, and then use the Select a Function list to click the function, if it appears.

You can also use these lists to select the function you want.

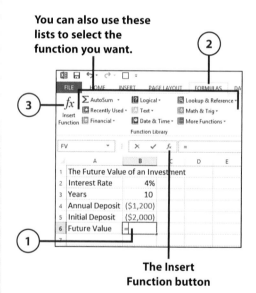

The Insert Function button

4. In the Or Select a Category list, select the category that contains your function. If you are not sure which category to choose, select All, instead.

5. In the Select a Function list, select the function you want to use.

6. Select OK. Excel displays the Function Arguments dialog box.

7. Enter the values or cell references you want to use for each argument. If you want to use a cell reference, note that you can enter it by tapping the cell.

8. Select OK. Excel inserts the function into the formula.

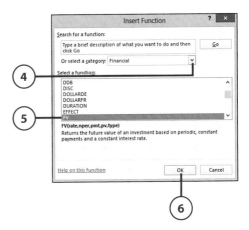

Required arguments are shown in bold type.

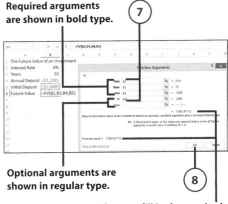

Optional arguments are shown in regular type.

After you fill in the required arguments, Excel displays the result of the function and the result of the cell formula.

Building a Table

Excel's forte is spreadsheet work, of course, but its row-and-column layout also makes it a natural database manager. In Excel, a *table* is a collection of related information with an organizational structure that makes it easy to find or extract data from its contents. Specifically, a table is a collection of cells that has the following properties:

- **Field**—A single type of information, such as a name, an address, or a phone number. In Excel tables, each column is a field.

- **Field value**—A single item in a field. In an Excel table, the field values are the individual cells.

- **Field name**—A unique name you assign to every table field (worksheet column). These names are always found in the first row of the table.

- **Record**—A collection of associated field values. In Excel tables, each row is a record.

Converting Cells to a Table

Excel has a number of commands that enable you to work efficiently with table data. To take advantage of these commands, you must convert your data from normal cells to a table.

1. Select any cell within the group of cells that you want to convert to a table.

2. Select the Insert tab.

3. Select Table. Excel displays the Create Table dialog box.

4. If your range has column headers in the top row (as it should), make sure the My Table Has Headers check box is selected.

5. Select OK. Excel converts the cells to a table.

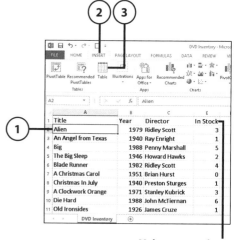

Make sure you have your field names in the top row.

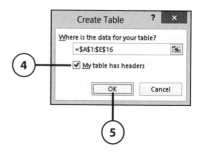

Selecting Table Elements

Before you can change the layout or formatting of a table, you need to select the part of the table you want to work with. Here are the techniques to use:

- **Select a cell**—Tap the cell.

- **Select two or more adjacent cells**—Select one of the cells and then drag the start and end selection handles to include the other cells.

- **Select a row**—Tap and hold any cell in the row, tap the drop-down arrow in the Mini Toolbar, tap Select, and then tap Table Row.

- **Select two or more adjacent rows**—Select at least one cell in each row, tap and hold the selection, tap the drop-down arrow in the Mini Toolbar, tap Select, and then tap Table Row.

- **Select a column**—Tap and hold any cell in the column, tap the drop-down arrow in the Mini Toolbar, tap Select, and then tap either Entire Table Column (to include the header) or Table Column Data (to exclude the header).

- **Select two or more adjacent columns**—Select at least one cell in each column, tap and hold any cell in the selection, tap the drop-down arrow in the Mini Toolbar, tap Select, and then tap either Entire Table Column (to include the headers) or Table Column Data (to exclude the headers).

Formatting a Table

To change the formatting of the table cells, you select the cells you want to work with and then use Excel's standard formatting tools (font, paragraph, and so on). For more table-specific formatting, you can use the Design tab.

1. Tap inside the table.

2. Select the Design tab.

3. Select the More button of the Table Styles gallery.

If you see the style you want to apply, you can select it without opening the Table Styles gallery.

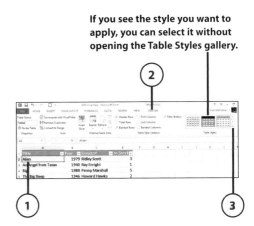

4. Select the style you want to apply to the table.

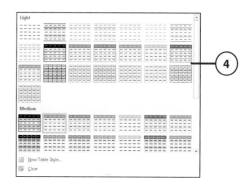

5. Select Header Row to toggle header formatting on and off for the first row. For example, in some styles the first row is given darker shading, top and bottom borders, and a bold font.

6. Select Total Row to toggle total formatting on and off for the bottom row.

7. Select Banded Rows to toggle alternating formatting for all the rows.

8. Select First Column to toggle special formatting on and off for the first column.

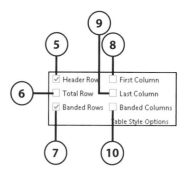

9. Select Last Column to toggle special formatting on and off for the last column.

10. Select Banded Columns to toggle alternating formatting for all the columns.

Creating a Custom Table Style

If the predefined table styles aren't quite what you're looking for, you can create a custom style to suit your needs. Select the More button of the Table Styles gallery, and then select New Table Style. In the New Table Style dialog box that opens, select a table element, select Format, and then use the controls to adjust the style's fonts, colors, borders, and more. Repeat for each table element you want to format, and then select OK.

Adding New Rows and Columns

When it's time to add more data to your table, Excel provides several tools that enable you to expand the table. If you're adding new items to the table, you need to add more rows; if you're adding more details to each item, you need to add more columns.

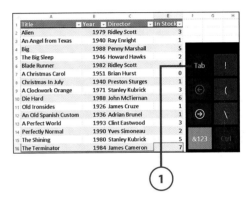

1. To add a new row at the end of the table, select the lower-right cell—that is, the last column of the last row—and press Tab.

2. Select the Home tab.

3. To add a new row above an existing row, position the active cell inside the existing row, select Insert, and then select Insert Table Rows Above.

4. To add a new column to the left of an existing column, position the active cell inside the existing column, select Insert, and then select Insert Table Columns to the Left.

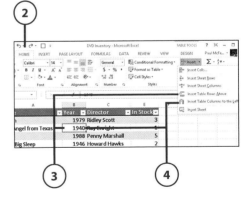

Adding Multiple Rows or Columns

If you want to insert multiple rows or columns, you can insert them all in one operation by first selecting the same number of existing rows or columns. For example, if you select two rows and then select Insert Table Rows Above, Excel inserts two rows above the selected rows.

Deleting Rows and Columns

If you find there's a part of your table you no longer need—for example, a row or a column—you can delete it. You can also delete multiple rows or columns.

1. Select the Home tab.

2. To delete a row, position the active cell inside the row, select Delete, and then select Delete Table Rows.

3. To delete a column, position the active cell inside the column, select Delete, and then select Delete Table Columns.

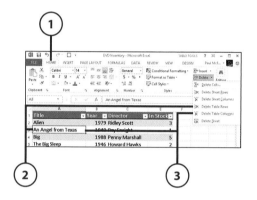

Selecting Elements for Deletion

If you want to delete a row or column, you need only tap anywhere inside that row or column. If you want to delete multiple rows or columns, then you need to select at least one cell in each row or column.

Sorting a Table

One of the advantages of using a table is that you can rearrange the records so that they're sorted alphabetically or numerically. Sorting enables you to view the data in order by customer name, account number, part number, or any other field.

Excel offers two kinds of sorts:

- **Ascending**—This type of sort arranges the items in a field from smallest to largest if the field is numeric, from A to Z if the field is text, and from oldest to newest if the field contains date or time data.

- **Descending**—This sort type arranges the items in a field from largest to smallest if the field contains numbers, from Z to A if the field contains text, and from newest to oldest if the field contains dates or times.

To indicate that a field is sorted, Excel adds an arrow to the field's Filter and Sort button (up for ascending; down for descending).

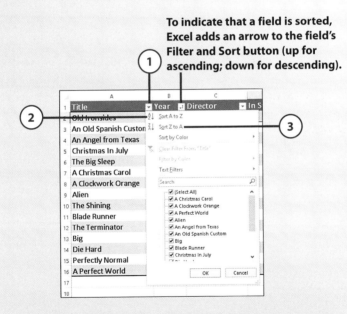

1. Select the Filter and Sort button (the drop-down arrow that appears beside the field header) for the field you want to use for the sort.

2. To sort a text field in ascending order, select Sort A to Z. If the field has numeric values, select Sort Smallest to Largest; if the field has date or time values, select Sort Oldest to Newest.

3. To sort a text field in descending order, select Sort Z to A. If the field has numeric values, select Sort Largest to Smallest; if the field has date or time values, select Sort Newest to Oldest.

Filtering a Table

One of the biggest problems with large tables is that it's often hard to find and extract the data you need. Sorting can help, but in the end, you're still working with the entire table. You need a way to define the data that you want to work with and then have Excel display only those records onscreen. This is called *filtering* your data, and Excel's Filter feature makes filtering out subsets of your data as easy as selecting check boxes from the *filter list*, a collection of the unique values in the field. When you deselect an item's check box, Excel temporarily hides all the table records that include that item in the field.

1. Select the Filter and Sort button for the field you want to use for the filter. Excel displays the field's filter list.

2. Deselect the check box for each item that you want to hide in the table.

3. Select OK.

To indicate that a field is filtered, Excel adds a funnel icon to the field's Filter and Sort button.

Quick filter

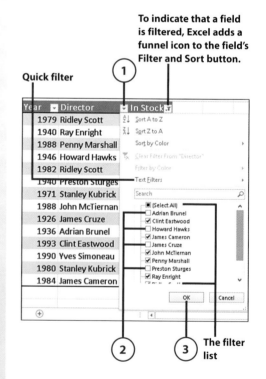

The filter list

FILTERING USING QUICK FILTERS

Besides allowing you to filter a table using a filter list, Excel also offers a set of *quick filters* that enable you to apply specific criteria. The quick filters you see depend on the data type of the field, but in each case, you access them by clicking a field's Filter and Sort button and then clicking one of the following commands:

- **Number Filters**—This command appears when you're working with a numeric field. It displays a submenu of filters, including Equals, Does Not Equal, Greater Than, Greater Than or Equal To, Less Than, Less Than or Equal To, Between, Top 10, Above Average, and Below Average.

- **Date Filters**—This command appears when you're working with a date field. It displays a submenu of filters, including Equals, Before, After, Between, Tomorrow, Today, Next Week, This Month, and Last Year.

- **Text Filters**—This command appears when you're working with a text field. It displays a submenu of filters, including Equals, Does Not Equal, Begins With, Ends With, Contains, and Does Not Contain.

In some cases, the quick filter doesn't require any input from you. For example, Above Average filters a table to show just the records that have a field value that's above the average for the field. However, most of the quick filters require some kind of input from you to complete the filter criteria. For example, Greater Than filters your table to show just the records that have a field value that's above some value that you specify.

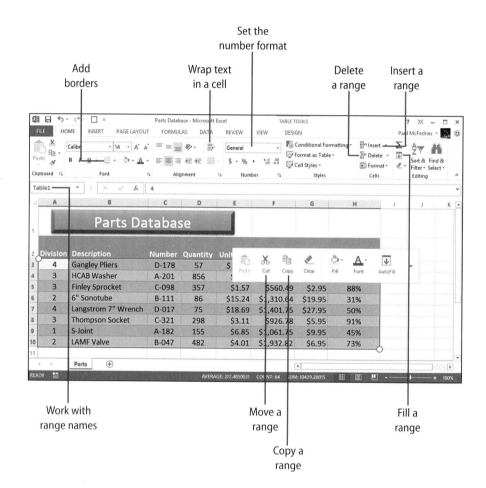

Set the
number format

Add
borders

Wrap text
in a cell

Delete
a range

Insert a
range

Work with
range names

Move a
range

Fill a
range

Copy a
range

In this chapter, you'll learn about various techniques for working with Excel ranges, including selecting, filling, copying, moving, deleting, naming, and formatting ranges.

8

→ Selecting ranges

→ Automatically filling a range with data

→ Copying, moving, inserting, and deleting ranges

→ Working with named ranges

→ Applying formatting to a range

Getting More Out of Excel Ranges

For small worksheets, working with individual cells doesn't usually present a problem. However, as your worksheets get larger, you'll find that performing operations cell by cell wastes both time and energy. To overcome this, Excel lets you work with multiple cells in a single operation. You can then move, copy, delete, or format the cells as a group.

A group of related cells is called a *range*. A range can be as small as a single cell and as large as an entire spreadsheet. Most ranges are rectangular groups of adjacent cells. Rectangular ranges, like individual cells, have an address, and this address is given in terms of *range coordinates*. Range coordinates have the form *UL:LR* where *UL* is the address of the cell in the upper-left corner of the range and *LR* is the address of the cell in the lower-right corner of the range (for example, A1:C5 and D7:G15).

This chapter shows you how to select ranges in Excel, and then how to work with ranges by filling them with data, copying and moving them, inserting and deleting them, applying names to them, and formatting them.

Selecting a Range

Ranges speed up your work by enabling you to perform operations or define functions on many cells at once instead of one at a time. For example, suppose you wanted to copy a large section of a worksheet to another file. If you worked on individual cells, you might have to perform the copy procedure dozens of times. However, by creating a range that covers the entire section, you could do it with a single copy command.

Similarly, suppose you wanted to know the average of a column of numbers running from B1 to B50. You could enter all 50 numbers as arguments in Excel's `AVERAGE()` function, but typing `AVERAGE(B1:B50)` is decidedly quicker.

Selecting a Range on a Touchscreen

If you're using Excel on a touchscreen PC, you can use gestures to select a range.

1. Tap the first cell in the range you want to select. This is usually the cell in the upper-left corner of the range.

2. Tap and drag the end selection handle down (if you want to include multiple rows in the range) or to the right (to include multiple columns). As you drag the handle, Excel selects the cells.

Start selection handle

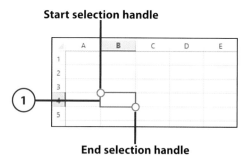

End selection handle

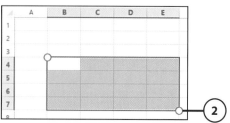

3. Tap the selection. Excel displays the Mini Toolbar, which you can use to format the selected range.

Mini Toolbar

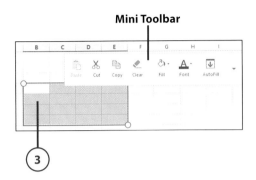

Selecting Entire Rows or Columns

To select an entire row, tap the row's heading. If you want to select multiple rows, tap and drag the selection handles left or right. To select an entire column, tap the column's heading. If you want to select multiple columns, tap and drag the selection handles up or down.

Working with Excel Ranges

Once you've selected a range, you need to do something with it. What can you do with a range? Well, perhaps a better question would be what *can't* you do with a range? You'll find that most of the Excel tasks you perform will involve ranges in some form or another. The next few sections, though, only show you some of the most common range chores, including filling, copying, moving, inserting, and deleting ranges.

Filling a Range with a Specific Value

You might occasionally need to fill a range with a particular value. For example, you might want to populate a range with a number for testing purposes, or you might need a value repeated across a range. Rather than type the value in by hand for each cell, you can use Excel's Fill tool to fill the range quickly.

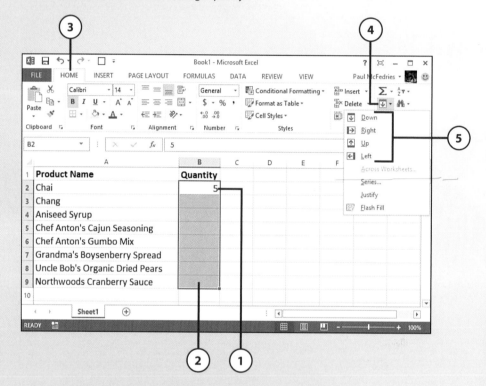

1. Type the value you want to repeat.

2. Select the range you want to fill, including the initial cell.

3. Select the Home tab.

4. Select Fill.

5. Select the appropriate command from the submenu that appears. For example, if you're filling a range down from the initial cell, select the Down command.

Keyboard Shortcut

Press Ctrl+D to select Home, Fill, Down; press Ctrl+R to select Home, Fill, Right. You can also select the range you want to fill, type the value or formula, and then press Ctrl+Enter.

Filling a Range with a Series of Values

Worksheets often use text series (such as January, February, March; or Sunday, Monday, Tuesday) and numeric series (such as 1, 3, 5; or 2013, 2014, 2015). Instead of entering these series by hand, you can use Excel's Series feature to create them automatically.

1. Select the first cell you want to use for the series, and enter the starting value. If you want to create a series out of a particular pattern (such as 2, 4, 6, and so on), fill in enough cells to define the pattern.

2. Select the entire range you want to fill.

3. Select Home.

4. Select Fill.

5. Select Series. Excel displays the Series dialog box.

6. If you selected a column, select the Columns option; otherwise, select the Rows option.

7. Use the Type group to select the type of series you want. Select the Date option if you're filling a series of dates. To fill in the range based on the pattern of the initial cell values you entered, select the AutoFill option. Use the Linear option to calculate the next series value by adding the step value (see step 9) to the preceding value in the series.

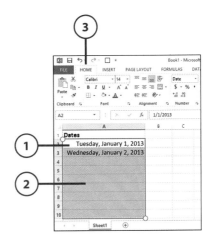

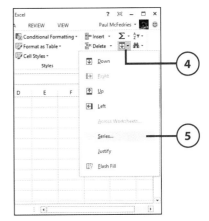

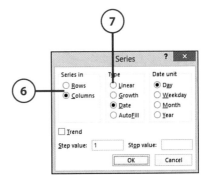

8. If you chose a Date series, select an option that specifies how you want the dates incremented: by Day, Weekday, Month, or Year.

9. If you chose a Linear or Date series type, enter a number in the Step Value box. This number is what Excel uses to increment each value in the series.

10. To place a limit on the series, enter the appropriate number in the Stop Value box.

11. Click OK. Excel fills in the series and returns you to the worksheet.

Making a Copy of a Range

The quickest way to become productive with Excel is to avoid reinventing your worksheets. If you have a formula that works, or a piece of formatting that you've put a lot of effort into, don't start from scratch if you need something similar. Instead, make a copy and then adjust the copy as necessary.

1. Select the range you want to copy.

2. Tap the selection to display the Mini Toolbar.

3. Tap Copy. (You can also select the Home tab's Copy command.) Excel copies the contents of the range to the Clipboard and displays a dashed border around the range.

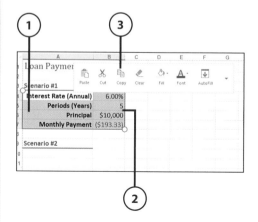

Keyboard Shortcut

You can also run the Copy command by pressing Ctrl+C.

4. Select the upper-left cell of the
   destination range.

5. Tap the cell again to display the
   Mini Toolbar.

6. Tap Paste. (You can also select
   Home and then select the top half
   of the Paste button.) Excel pastes
   a copy of the range from the
   Clipboard to your destination.

Keyboard Shortcut

You can also run the Paste command by pressing Ctrl+V.

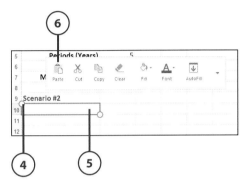

DON'T OVERWRITE EXISTING CELLS

Before copying a range to another area, look at the destination area and
make sure you won't be overwriting any nonblank cells. Remember that you
can use the Undo command if you accidentally destroy some data. If you
want to insert the range among some existing cells without overwriting
existing data, see the "Inserting a Range" section later in this chapter.

>>>Go Further

Moving a Range

If a range is in the wrong section of a worksheet, you can move the range to the sheet area that you prefer.

1. Select the range you want to move.

2. Tap the selection to display the Mini Toolbar.

3. Tap Cut. (You can also select the Home tab's Cut command.) Excel places the contents of the range on the Clipboard and displays a dashed border around the range.

Keyboard Shortcut

You can also run the Cut command by pressing Ctrl+X.

---

4. Select the upper-left cell of the destination range.

5. Tap the cell again to display the Mini Toolbar.

6. Tap Paste. (You can also select Home and then select the top half of the Paste button.) Excel pastes the range data from the Clipboard to the destination and deletes the original text.

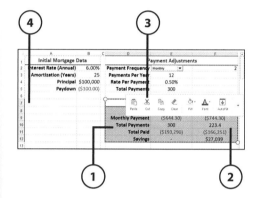

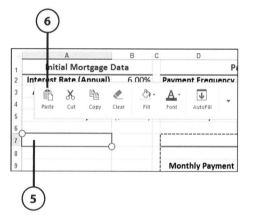

Inserting a Range

When you begin a worksheet, you use up rows and columns sequentially as you add data and formulas. Invariably, however, you'll need to go back and add in some values or labels that you forgot or that you need for another part of the worksheet. When this happens, you need to insert ranges into your spreadsheet to make room for your new information.

1. Select the range where you want the new range to appear. If you're inserting a horizontal range, select the cells above which you want the new range to appear. If you're inserting a vertical range, select the cells to the left of which you want the new range to appear.

2. Select the Home tab.

3. Drop down the Insert menu.

4. Select Insert Cells. The Insert dialog box opens.

5. Select the option that fits how you want Excel to adjust the existing cells to accommodate your inserted range. For example, if you're inserting a horizontal range, select Shift Cells Down to make horizontal room for your new range. Similarly, if you're inserting a vertical range, select Shift Cells Right to make vertical room for your new range.

6. Select OK. Excel inserts the range and shifts the existing cells accordingly.

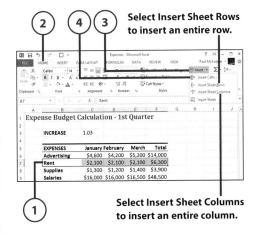

Select Insert Sheet Rows to insert an entire row.

Select Insert Sheet Columns to insert an entire column.

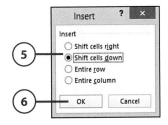

Deleting a Range

When you're building a worksheet, you often have to remove old or unnecessary data, and that requires you to delete ranges. It's often easiest to delete an entire row or column, but in some worksheets, you may need to delete only a single cell or a range of cells so as not to disturb the arrangement of surrounding data.

1. Select the range you want to delete.

2. Select the Home tab.

3. Drop down the Delete menu.

4. Select Delete Cells. The Insert dialog box opens.

5. Select the option that fits how you want Excel to adjust the existing cells to accommodate your inserted range. For example, if you're inserting a horizontal range, select Shift Cells Down to make horizontal room for your new range. Similarly, if you're inserting a vertical range, select Shift Cells Right to make vertical room for your new range.

6. Select OK. Excel inserts the range and shifts the existing cells accordingly.

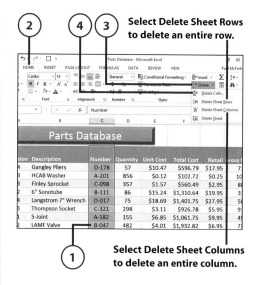

Select Delete Sheet Rows to delete an entire row.

Select Delete Sheet Columns to delete an entire column.

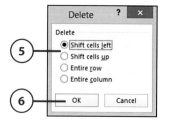

Working with Range Names

Working with multiple cells as a range is much easier than working with the cells individually, but range coordinates are not very intuitive. For example, if you see a formula that uses the function AVERAGE(A1:A25), knowing what the range A1:A25 represents is impossible unless you look at the range itself.

You can make ranges more intuitive using *range names*, which are labels that you assign to a single cell or to a range of cells. With a name defined, you can use it in place of the range coordinates. For example, assigning the name ClassMarks to a range such as A1:A25 immediately clarifies the purpose of a function such as AVERAGE(ClassMarks).

Excel also makes range names easy to work with by automatically adjusting the coordinates associated with a range name if you move the range or if you insert or delete rows or columns within the range.

Range names are generally quite flexible, but you need to follow a few restrictions and guidelines:

- The range name can be no longer than 255 characters.

- The range name must begin with either a letter or the underscore character (_). For the rest of the name, you can use any combination of characters, numbers, or symbols, except spaces. For multiple-word names, separate the words by using the underscore character or by mixing case (for example, August_Expenses or AugustExpenses). Excel doesn't distinguish between uppercase and lowercase letters in range names.

- Don't use cell addresses (such as Q1) or any of the operator symbols (such as +, −, *, /, <, >, and &) because they could cause confusion if you use the name in a formula.

- Keep your names as short as possible to reduce typing, but long enough that the name retains some of its meaning. NetProfit13 is faster to type than Net_Profit_For_Fiscal_Year_2013, and it's certainly clearer than the more cryptic NetPft13.

The Name box to the left of Excel's Formula bar usually just shows you the address of the active cell. However, the Name box also comes with two extra features that are quite useful when you are working with range names: After you define a name, it appears in the Name box whenever you select the range; the Name box contains a list of the defined names. To select a named range quickly, drop down the list and click the name you want.

Naming a Range

The Name box is also the quickest way to define a range name.

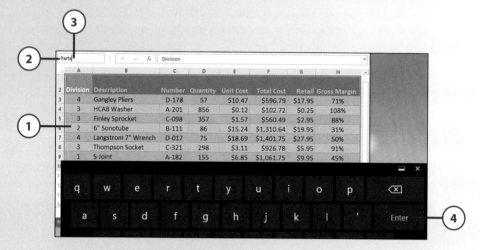

1. Select the range you want to name.

2. Tap inside the Name box to display the insertion point.

3. Type the name you want to use.

4. Press Enter. Excel defines the new name automatically.

>>>Go Further

NAMING A RANGE USING WORKSHEET TEXT

If you have a few ranges to name—for example, a series of rows or columns—you can speed things up by using the worksheet text adjacent to each range as the range name. To try this, first select the range of cells you want to name, including the appropriate text cells that you want to use as the range names. Select the Formulas tab and then select Create from Selection. Excel displays the Create Names from Selection dialog box and Excel guesses where the text for the range name is located and activates the appropriate check box (such as Top Row or Left Column). If this isn't the check box you want, deselect it and then select the appropriate one. Click OK.

Formatting a Range

Your worksheets must produce the correct answers, of course, so most of your Excel time should be spent on getting your data and formulas entered accurately. However, you also need to spend some time formatting your work, particularly if other people will be viewing or working with the spreadsheet. Labels, data, and formula results that have been augmented with fonts, borders, alignments, numeric formats, and other formatting are almost always easier to read and understand than unformatted sheets.

Learning About Data Formats

One of the best ways to improve the readability of worksheets is to display data in a format that is logical, consistent, and straightforward. Formatting currency amounts with leading dollar signs, percentages with trailing percent signs, and large numbers with commas are a few of the ways you can improve your spreadsheet style.

When you enter numbers in a worksheet, Excel removes any leading or trailing zeros. For example, if you enter 0123.4500, Excel displays 123.45. The exception to this rule occurs when you enter a number that's wider than the cell. In this case, Excel usually expands the width of the column to fit the number. However, in some cases, Excel tailors the number to fit the cell by rounding off some decimal places. For example, the number 123.45678 might be displayed as 123.4568. Note that, in this case, the number is changed for display purposes only; Excel still retains the original number internally.

When you create a worksheet, each cell uses this format, known as the general number format, by default. If you want your numbers to appear differently, you can choose from among Excel's six categories of numeric formats:

- **Number**—The Number format has three components: the number of decimal places (0–30), whether the thousands separator (,) is used, and how negative numbers are displayed. For negative numbers, you can display the number with a leading minus sign, in red, surrounded by parentheses or in red surrounded by parentheses.

- **Currency**—The Currency format is similar to the Number format, except that the thousands separator is always used and the number appears with a leading dollar sign ($).

- **Accounting**—The Accounting format is the same as the Currency format, except Excel displays the dollar sign ($) flush left in the cell. All negative entries are displayed surrounded by parentheses.

- **Percentage**—The Percentage format displays the number multiplied by 100, with a percent sign (%) to the right of the number. For example, .506 is displayed as 50.6%. You can display 0–30 decimal places.

- **Fraction**—The Fraction format enables you to express decimal quantities as fractions.

- **Scientific**—The Scientific format displays the most significant number to the left of the decimal, 2–30 decimal places to the right of the decimal, and then the exponent. So, 123000 is displayed as 1.23E+05.

The quickest way to format numbers is to specify the format as you enter your data. For example, if you begin a dollar amount with a dollar sign ($), Excel automatically formats the number as Currency. Similarly, if you type a percent sign (%) after a number, Excel automatically formats the number as Percentage. Here are a few more examples of this technique. Note that you can enter a negative value using either the minus sign (-) or parentheses.

Number Entered	Number Displayed	Format Used
$1234.567	$1,234.57	Currency
($1234.5)	($1,234.50)	Currency
10%	10%	Percentage
123E+02	1.23E+04	Scientific
5 3/4	5 3/4	Fraction
0 3/4	3/4	Fraction
3/4	4-Mar	Date

Entering a Simple Fraction

Excel interprets a simple fraction such as 3/4 as a date (March 4, in this case). Always include a leading zero, followed by a space, if you want to enter a simple fraction from the Formula bar.

If you include dates or times in your worksheets, you need to make sure that they're presented in a readable, unambiguous format. For example, most people would interpret the date 8/5/13 as August 5, 2013. However, in some countries, this date would mean May 8, 2013. Similarly, if you use the time

2:45, do you mean AM or PM? To avoid these kinds of problems, you can use Excel's built-in date and time formats, listed in Table 8.1.

Table 8.1   Excel's Date and Time Formats

Format	Display
m/d	8/3
m/d/yy	8/3/13
mm/dd/yy	08/03/13
d-mmm	3-Aug
d-mmm-yy	3-Aug-13
dd-mmm-yy	03-Aug-13
mmm-yy	Aug-13
mmmm-yy	August-13
mmmm d, yyyy	August 3, 2013
h:mm AM/PM	3:10 PM
h:mm:ss AM/PM	3:10:45 PM
h:mm	15:10
h:mm:ss	15:10:45
mm:ss.0	10:45.7
[h]:[mm]:[ss]	25:61:61
m/d/yy h:mm AM/PM	8/23/13 3:10 PM
m/d/yy h:mm	8/23/13 15:10

You use the same methods to select date and time formats that you used for numeric formats. In particular, you can specify the date and time format as you input your data. For example, entering **Jan-13** automatically formats the cell with the mmm-yy format. You also have the following commands available:

- **Short Date**—Choose this command to display a date using the mm/dd/yyyy format.

- **Long Date**—Choose this command to display a date using the dddd, mmmm dd, yyyy.

- **Time**—Choose this command to display a time using the hh:mm:ss AM/PM format.

Applying a Numeric or Date Format

Specifying the numeric format as you enter a number is fast and efficient because Excel guesses the format you want to use. Unfortunately, Excel sometimes guesses wrong (for example, interpreting a simple fraction as a date). In any case, you don't have access to all the available formats (for example, displaying negative dollar amounts in red). To overcome these limitations, you can select your numeric formats from a list.

1. Select the cell or range of cells to which you want to apply the new format.

2. Select the Home tab.

3. Drop down the Number Format list. Excel displays its built-in formats.

4. Select the format you want to use. Excel applies the numeric format to the cell or range.

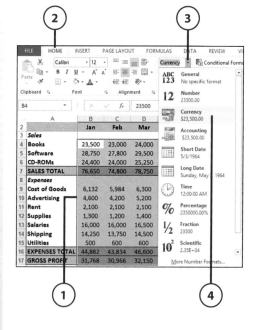

Customizing Numeric Formats

To get a bit more control over the numeric formats, drop down the Number Format list and then select More Number Formats. The Number tab of the Format Cells dialog box enables you to specify the number of decimal places, the currency symbol, and more.

Controlling the Number of Decimal Places

You can make your numeric values easier to read and interpret by adjusting the number of decimal places that Excel displays. For example, you might want to ensure that all dollar-and-cent values show two decimal places, while dollar-only values show no decimal places. You can either decrease or increase the number of decimal places that Excel displays.

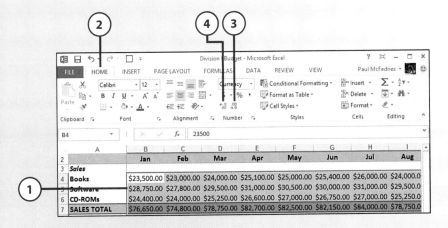

1. Select the range you want to format.

2. Select the Home tab.

3. In the Number group, select the Decrease Decimal button. Excel decreases the number of decimal places by one.

4. To increase the number of decimal places, instead, select the Increase Decimal button.

Handling Multiple Numbers of Decimal Places

How does Excel handle situations in which the selected range has values that display different numbers of decimal places? In this case, Excel uses the value that has the most displayed decimal places as the basis for formatting all the values. For example, if the selected range has values that display zero, one, two, or four decimal places, Excel uses the value with four decimal places as the basis. If you click Decrease Decimal, Excel displays every value with three decimal places; if you click Increase Decimal, Excel displays every value with five decimal places.

Resizing Columns

You can use column width adjustments to improve the appearance of your worksheet in a number of different ways. For example, if you're faced with a truncated text entry or a number that Excel shows as ######, you can enlarge the column so the entry can appear in full.

1. Select at least one cell in each column you want to resize.

2. Select the Home tab.

3. Select Format.

4. Select Column Width. Excel displays the Column Width dialog box.

5. In the Column Width text box, type the width you want.

6. Select OK. Excel sets the column width and returns you to the worksheet.

Resizing a Column with a Mouse

If you have a mouse, move the mouse pointer to the column header area and position the pointer at the right edge of the column you want to resize. The mouse pointer changes to a two-headed horizontal arrow with a vertical bar in the middle. Either drag the edge of the column right (to increase the width) or left (to decrease the width), or double-click to automatically size the column to its widest entry.

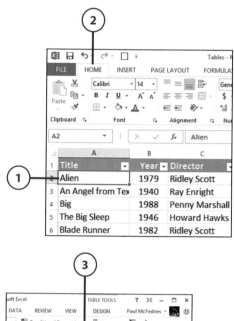

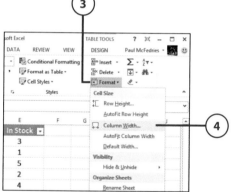

Resizing Rows

Although Excel normally adjusts row heights automatically to accommodate the tallest font in a row, you can make your own height adjustments to give your worksheet more breathing room or to reduce the amount of space taken up by unused rows.

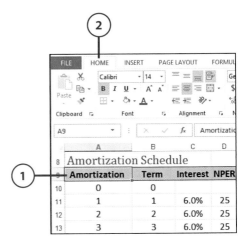

1. Select at least one cell in each row you want to resize.

2. Select the Home tab.

3. Select Format.

4. Select Row Height. Excel displays the Row Height dialog box.

5. In the Row Height text box, type the height you want.

6. Select OK. Excel sets the row height and returns you to the worksheet.

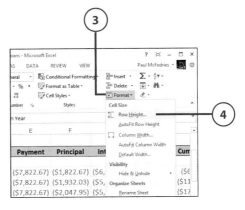

Resizing a Row with a Mouse

If you have a mouse, move the mouse pointer to the row header area and position the pointer at the bottom edge of the row you want to resize. The mouse pointer changes to a two-headed vertical arrow with a horizontal bar in the middle. Either drag the edge of the row up (to increase the height) or down (to decrease the height), or double-click to automatically size the row to its tallest entry.

Adding Borders

Excel lets you place borders of patterns around your worksheet cells or ranges. This is useful for enclosing different parts of the worksheet, defining data entry areas, and separating headings from data. You can also use borders to make a range easier to read. For example, if a range has totals on the bottom row, you can add a border above the totals.

1. Select the range you want to format.

2. Select the Home tab.

3. Select Borders. Excel displays a list of border types.

4. Select the border type you want to use. Excel applies the border to the range.

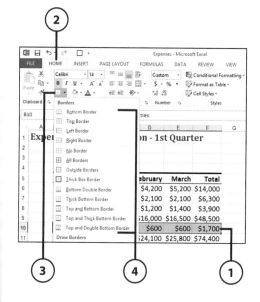

Wrapping Text Within a Cell

If you type more text in a cell than can fit horizontally, Excel either displays the text over the next cell if that cell is empty or displays only part of the text if the next cell contains data. To prevent Excel from showing only truncated cell data, you can format the cell to wrap text within the cell. Excel then increases the height of the row to ensure that all the text is displayed.

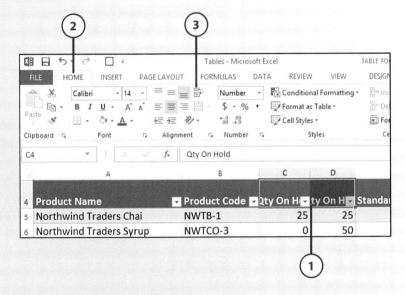

1. Select the range you want to format.

2. Click the Home tab.

3. In the Alignment group, click Wrap Text. Excel wraps the text as needed within each cell in the range and then increases the height of the row to ensure that all the text is displayed.

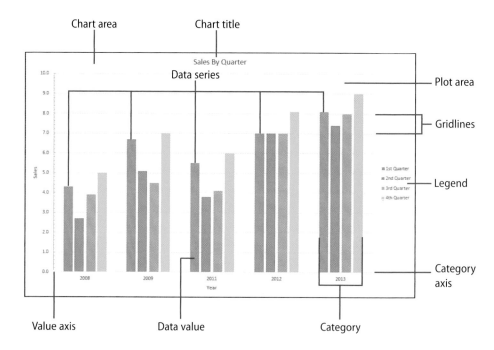

In this chapter, you'll learn about creating, customizing, and formatting charts to help visualize your Excel data.

→ Converting Excel data into a chart

→ Working with Excel's different chart types

→ Moving, resizing, and changing the layout of a chart

→ Selecting and formatting chart elements

→ Adding chart titles, a legend, and data labels

Visualizing Excel Data with Charts

One of the best ways to analyze your worksheet data—or get your point across to other people—is to display your data visually in a chart. Excel gives you tremendous flexibility when creating charts: It enables you to place charts in separate documents or directly on the worksheet itself. Not only that, but you have dozens of different chart formats to choose from, and if none of Excel's built-in formats is just right, you can further customize these charts to suit your needs.

Creating a Chart

When plotting your worksheet data, you have two basic options: You can create an embedded chart that sits on top of your worksheet and can be moved, sized, and formatted; or you can create a separate chart sheet. Whether you choose to embed your charts or store them in separate sheets, the charts are linked with the worksheet data. Any changes you make to the data are automatically updated in the chart.

Before getting to the specifics of creating a chart, you should familiarize yourself with some basic chart terminology:

- **Category**—A grouping of data values on the category horizontal axis.

- **Category axis**—The axis (usually the x-axis) that contains the category groupings.

- **Chart area**—The area on which the chart is drawn.

- **Data marker**—A symbol that represents a specific data value. The symbol used depends on the chart type. In a column chart, for example, each column is a marker.

- **Data series**—A collection of related data values. Normally, the marker for each value in a series has the same pattern.

- **Data value**—A single piece of data. Also called a *data point*.

- **Gridlines**—Optional horizontal and vertical extensions of the axis tick marks. These make data values easier to read.

- **Legend**—A guide that shows the colors, patterns, and symbols used by the markers for each data series.

- **Plot area**—The area bounded by the category and value axes. It contains the data points and gridlines.

- **Tick mark**—A small line that intersects the category axis or the value axis. It marks divisions in the chart's categories or scales.

- **Value axis**—The axis (usually the y-axis) that contains the data values.

Creating an Embedded Chart

An *embedded* chart is one that appears on the same worksheet as the data that it's based on. Creating an embedded chart is by far the easiest way to build a chart in Excel because the basic technique requires just a few steps.

1. Select the range you want to plot, including the row and column labels if there are any. Make sure that no blank rows are between the column labels and the data.

2. Select Insert.

3. In the Charts group, drop down the list for the chart type you want. Excel displays a gallery of chart types.

4. Select a chart type. Excel embeds the chart.

If you're not sure which chart type to use, select Recommended Charts.

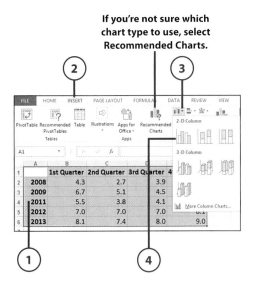

Creating a Chart in a Separate Sheet

If you don't want a chart taking up space in a worksheet, or if you want to print a chart on its own, you can create a separate chart sheet.

1. Select the range you want to plot, including the row and column labels if there are any. Make sure that no blank rows are between the column labels and the data.

2. Tap and hold (or right-click) the tab of the worksheet before which you want the chart sheet to appear.

3. Select Insert. Excel displays the Insert dialog box.

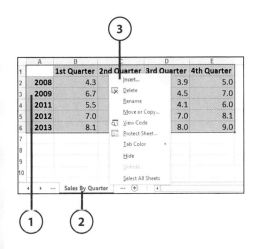

4. Select Chart.

5. Select OK. Excel creates the chart sheet and adds a default chart.

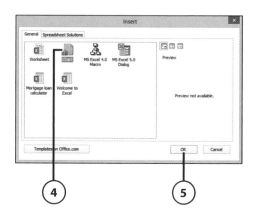

Keyboard Shortcut

To insert a chart in a separate sheet using the keyboard, select the data you want to chart and then press F11.

Working with Charts

Once you've created a chart, Excel offers various tools for working with the chart, including changing the chart type, moving and resizing the chart, and changing the chart layout. The next few sections provide the details.

Understanding Excel's Chart Types

To help you choose the chart type that best presents your data, the following list provides brief descriptions of all of Excel's chart types:

- **Area chart**—An *area chart* shows the relative contributions over time that each data series makes to the whole picture. The smaller the area a data series takes up, the smaller its contribution to the whole.

- **Bar chart**—A *bar chart* compares distinct items or shows single items at distinct intervals. A bar chart is laid out with categories along the vertical axis and values along the horizontal axis. This format lends itself to competitive comparisons because categories appear to be "ahead" or "behind."

- **Column chart**—Like a bar chart, a *column chart* compares distinct items or shows single items at distinct intervals. However, a column chart is laid out with categories along the horizontal axis and values along the vertical axis (as are most Excel charts). This format is best suited for comparing items over time. Excel offers various column chart formats, including *stacked columns*. A stacked column chart is similar to an area chart; series values are stacked on top of each other to show the relative contributions of each series. Although an area chart is useful for showing the flow of the relative contributions over time, a stacked column chart is better for showing the contributions at discrete intervals.

- **Line chart**—A *line chart* shows how a data series changes over time. The category (x) axis usually represents a progression of even increments (such as days or months), and the series points are plotted on the value (y) axis. Excel offers several stock chart formats, including an Open, High, Low, Close chart (also called a *candlestick chart*), which is useful for plotting stock-market prices.

- **Pie chart**—A *pie chart* shows the proportion of the whole that is contributed by each value in a single data series. The whole is represented as a circle (the "pie"), and each value is displayed as a proportional "slice" of the circle.

- **Radar chart**—A *radar chart* makes comparisons within a data series and between data series relative to a center point. Each category is shown with a value axis extending from the center point. To understand this concept, think of a radar screen in an airport control tower. The tower itself is the central point, and the radar radiates a beam (a value axis). When the radar makes contact with a plane, a blip appears onscreen. In a radar chart, this data point is shown with a data marker.

- **XY (scatter) chart**—An *XY chart* (also called a scatter chart) shows the relationship between numeric values in two different data series. It also can plot a series of data pairs in x,y coordinate. An XY chart is a variation of the line chart in which the category axis is replaced by a second value axis. You can use XY charts for plotting items such as survey data, mathematical functions, and experimental results.

- **Bubble chart**—A *bubble chart* is similar to an XY chart, except that it uses three data series, and in the third series the individual plot points are displayed as bubbles (the larger the value, the larger the bubble).

- **Doughnut chart**—A *doughnut chart*, like a pie chart, shows the proportion of the whole that is contributed by each value in a data series. The advantage of a doughnut chart, however, is that you can plot multiple data series. (A pie chart can handle only a single series.)

- **3-D charts**—In addition to the various 2-D chart types presented so far, Excel also offers 3-D charts. Because they're striking, 3-D charts are suitable for presentations, flyers, and newsletters. (If you need a chart to help with data analysis, or if you just need a quick chart to help you visualize your data, you're probably better off with the simpler 2-D charts.) Most of the 3-D charts are just the 2-D versions with an enhanced 3-D effect. However, some 3-D charts enable you to look at your data in new ways. For example, some 3-D area chart types enable you to show separate area plots for each data series (something a 2-D area chart can't do). In this variation, the emphasis isn't on the relative contribution of each series to the whole; rather, it's on the relative differences among the series.

Changing the Chart Type

If you feel that the current chart type is not showing your data in the best way, you can change the chart type. This enables you to experiment not only with the 10 different chart types offered by Excel, but also with its nearly 100 chart type configurations.

1. Tap the chart to select it.

2. Select the Design tab.

3. Select Change Chart Type. The Change Chart Type dialog box opens.

4. Select the chart type you want to use. Excel displays the chart type configurations.

5. Select the general configuration you want to use.

6. Select the specific configuration you want to use.

7. Select OK.

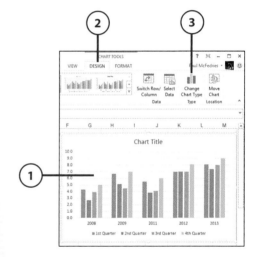

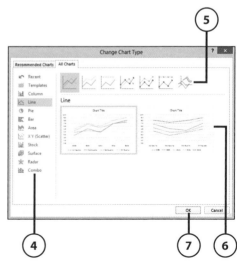

CREATING A CHART TEMPLATE

Once you've changed the chart type, as described in this section, and performed other chart-related chores such as applying titles, adding labels, and choosing a layout (described later in this chapter), you might want to repeat the same settings on another chart. Rather than repeating the same procedures on the second chart, you can make your life easier by saving the original chart as a chart template. This enables you to then build the second chart (and any subsequent charts) based on this template. To save the chart as a template, tap and hold (or right-click) the chart's plot area or background, drop down the Mini Toolbar's menu, and then select Save as Template. Type a name for the template and then select Save. To reuse the template, follow steps 1 to 3 in this section, select Templates, select your template, and then select OK.

Moving a Chart

You can move a chart to another part of the worksheet. This is useful if the chart is blocking the worksheet data or if you want the chart to appear in a particular part of the worksheet.

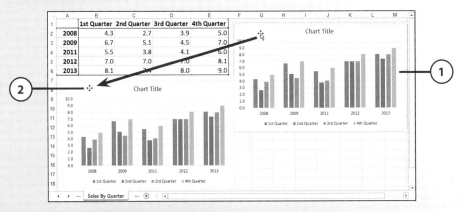

1. Tap the chart to select it.
2. Tap and drag an empty section of the chart to the location you want. As you drag, Excel moves the chart.

Dragging an Edge

If you drag a chart object such as the plot area or the chart title, you'll only move that object, not the entire chart. If you're having trouble finding a place to drag, try dragging any edge of the chart. However, try to avoid dragging any of the selection handles (see the next section), or you'll just resize the chart.

MOVING A CHART TO A SEPARATE SHEET

In the "Creating a Chart in a Separate Sheet" section, earlier in this chapter, you learned how to create a new chart in a separate sheet. If your chart already exists on a worksheet, you can move it to a new sheet. Tap the chart, select the Design tab, and then select Move Chart to open the Move Chart dialog box. Select the New Sheet option, use the New Sheet text box to type a name for the new sheet, and then select OK.

Resizing a Chart

You can resize a chart. For example, if you find that the chart is difficult to read, making the chart bigger often solves the problem. Similarly, if the chart takes up too much space on the worksheet, you can make it smaller.

1. Tap the chart. Excel displays a border around the chart, which includes selection handles on the corners and sides.

2. Tap and drag a selection handle until the chart is the size you want. When you release the screen, Excel resizes the chart.

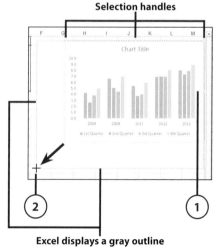

Selection handles

Excel displays a gray outline of the new chart size.

Changing the Chart Layout and Style

You can quickly format your chart by applying a different chart layout. The chart layout includes elements such as the titles, data labels, legend, and gridlines. The Quick Layouts feature in Excel enables you to apply these elements in different combinations in just a few steps. You can also apply a chart style, which governs the formatting applied to the chart background, data markers, gridlines, and more.

1. Tap the chart.

2. Select the Design tab.

3. Select Quick Layout.

4. Select the layout you want to use.

5. Select the More button in the Chart Styles section. Excel displays the Chart Styles gallery.

6. Select the style you want to apply.

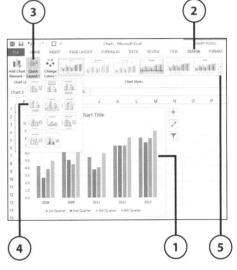

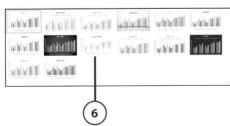

Working with Chart Elements

An Excel chart is composed of elements such as axes, data markers, gridlines, and text, each with its own formatting options. In the rest of this chapter, you'll learn how to work with several of these elements, including titles, legends, and data markers.

Selecting Chart Elements

Before you can format a chart element, you need to select it.

1. Tap the chart.

2. Select the Format tab.

3. Drop down the Chart Elements list to display a list of all the elements in the current chart.

4. Select the element you want to work with.

Selecting Chart Elements Directly

You can also select many chart elements directly by tapping them.

Formatting Chart Elements

If you want to format a particular chart element, the Format tab offers several options for most chart elements. However, the bulk of your element formatting chores will take place in the Format task pane, the layout of which depends on the selected element.

1. Select the chart element you want to format.

2. Select the Format tab.

3. Select Format Selection. Excel displays the Format task pane.

4. Select the Options tab to work with the element's settings.

5. Select the Size & Properties tab to control the size of the element and set the element's properties.

6. Select the Effects tab to control element formatting such as shadows, glow effects, soft edges, and 3-D effects.

7. Select the Fill & Line tab to control formatting such as the element's background color and the color and style of its borders.

Format Task Pane Tabs

Not all chart elements display all of the tabs mentioned here.

You can use the options in the Shape Styles group to apply formatting to most chart elements.

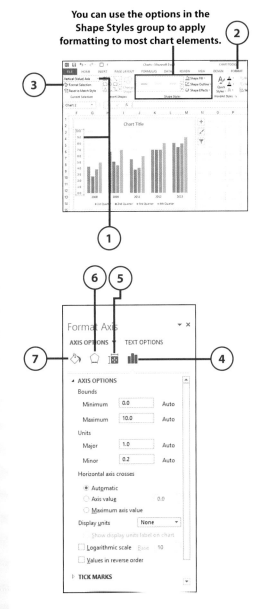

Adding Titles

Excel enables you to add four kinds of titles: the *chart title* is the overall chart title and you use it to provide a brief description that puts the chart into context; the *category (X) axis title* appears below the category axis, and you use it to provide a brief description of the category items; the *value (Y) axis title* appears to the left of the value axis, and you use it to provide a brief description of the value items; and the *value (Z) axis title* appears beside the z-axis in a 3-D chart, and you use it to provide a brief description of the z-axis items.

1. Tap the chart.

2. Select the Design tab.

3. Select Add Chart Element.

4. Select Chart Title.

5. Select Above Chart. Excel adds the title box.

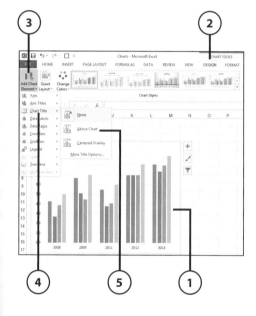

6. Type the title.

7. Select Add Chart Element.

8. Select Axis Titles.

9. Select Primary Horizontal. Excel adds the title box.

10. Type the title.

11. Select Add Chart Element.

12. Select Axis Titles.

13. Select Primary Vertical. Excel adds the title box.

14. Type the title.

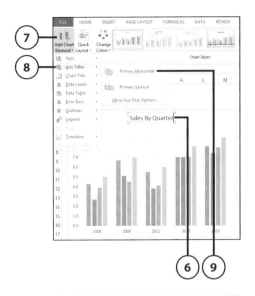

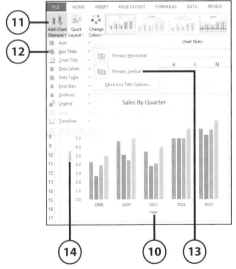

Adding a Chart Legend

If your chart includes multiple data series, you should add a legend to explain the series markers. Doing so makes your chart more readable and makes it easier for others to distinguish each series.

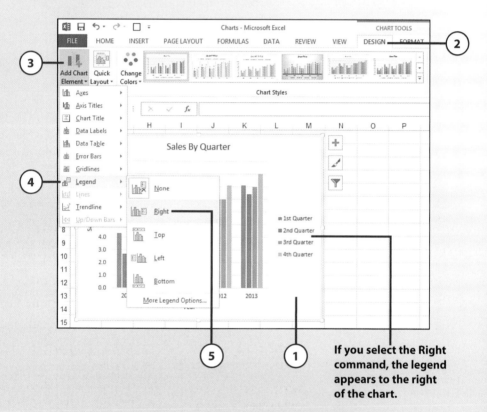

If you select the Right command, the legend appears to the right of the chart.

1. Tap the chart.

2. Select the Design tab.

3. Select Add Chart Element.

4. Select Legend.

5. Select the position you want to use for the legend. Excel adds the legend.

Adding Data Marker Labels

You can make your chart easier to read by adding data labels. A *data label* is a small text box that appears in or near a data marker and displays the value of that data point.

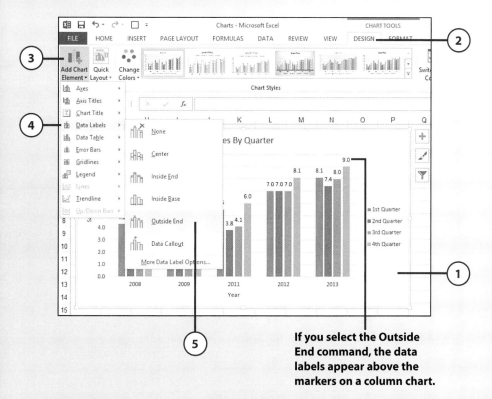

If you select the Outside End command, the data labels appear above the markers on a column chart.

1. Tap the chart.
2. Select the Design tab.
3. Select Add Chart Element.
4. Select Data Labels.
5. Select the position you want to use for the data labels. Excel adds the labels to the chart.

Data Label Positions

The data label position options you see depend on the chart type. For example, with a column chart you can place the data labels within or above each column, and for a line chart you can place the labels to the left or right, or above or below, the data marker.

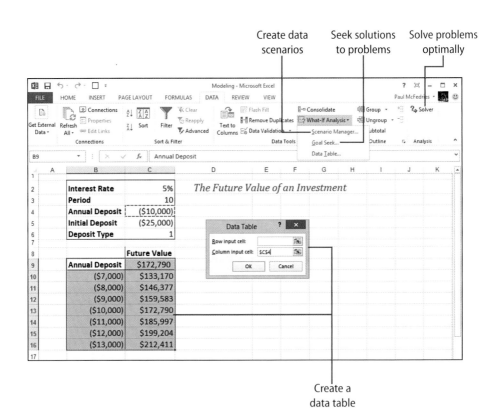

Create data scenarios

Seek solutions to problems

Solve problems optimally

Create a data table

In this chapter, you'll learn about various ways to analyze your Excel data, including using data tables, Goal Seek, scenarios, and the Solver add-in.

→ Understanding what-if analysis
→ Setting up one- and two-input data tables
→ Solving problems with Goal Seek
→ Saving model input values as scenarios
→ Optimally solving problems with Solver

Analyzing Excel Data

At times, it's not enough to simply enter data in a worksheet, build a few formulas, and add a little formatting to make things presentable. You're often called on to divine some inner meaning from the jumble of numbers and formula results that litter your workbooks. In other words, you need to *analyze* your data to see what nuggets of understanding you can unearth. In Excel, this means using the program's data analysis tools. This chapter looks at a few of those tools and some analytic techniques that have many uses. You'll learn how to use Excel's numerous methods for what-if analysis, how to wield Excel's useful Goal Seek tool, how to create scenarios, and more.

Applying What-If Analysis

What-if analysis is perhaps the most basic method for interrogating your worksheet data. With what-if analysis, you first calculate a formula D, based on the input from variables A, B, and C. You then say, "What if I change variable A? Or B or C? What happens to the result?"

For example, suppose you have a worksheet that uses the FV () function to calculate the future value of an investment based on five variables: the interest rate, period, annual deposit, initial deposit, and deposit type. Now the questions begin:

- What if you changed the interest rate from 5% to 6%?

- What if you deposited $8,000 per year instead of $10,000?

- What if you reduced the initial deposit?

Answering these questions is a straightforward matter of changing the appropriate variables and watching the effect on the result. However, the problem with modifying formula variables is that you see only a single result at one time. If you're interested in studying the effect a range of values has on the formula, you need to set up a *data table*. In the investment analysis worksheet, for example, suppose that you want to see the future value of the investment with the annual deposit varying between $7,000 and $13,000. You could just enter these values in a row or column and then create the appropriate formulas. Setting up a data table, however, is much easier, as the following sections show.

>>>Go Further

In the sections that follow, you'll notice that Excel modifies your cell reference to include dollar signs ($) before both the column letter and row number (for example, C4). This is known as the *absolute reference format*, and it means that the cell address does not change as Excel applies the input values. Absolute cell references are also useful in regular worksheet situations where you want a particular cell address to remain constant even when you move the formula or fill a range with a formula.

Creating a One-Input Data Table

A *one-input* data table applies multiple values into a single input cell.

1. Add to the worksheet the values you want to input into the formula.

Entering the Input Values

When you're adding the input values, you have two choices. If you want to enter the values in a column, start the column one cell down and one cell to the left of the cell containing the formula. Alternatively, if you want to enter the values in a row, start the row one cell up and one cell to the right of the formula.

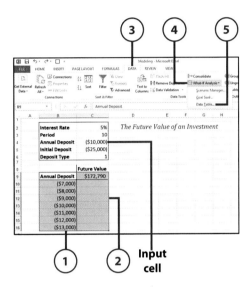

Input cell

2. Select the range that includes the input values and the formula.

3. Select the Data tab.

4. Select What-If Analysis.

5. Select Data Table. Excel displays the Data Table dialog box.

6. If the input values are in a column, enter the input cell's address in the Column Input Cell text box.

7. Select OK.

If you entered the input values in a row, use the Row Input Cell text box to enter the address of the input cell.

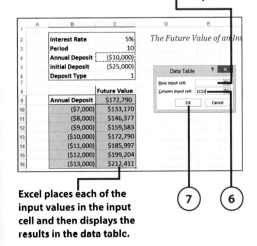

Excel places each of the input values in the input cell and then displays the results in the data table.

>> Go Further

EDITING A DATA TABLE

If you want to make changes to the data table, you can edit the formula as well as the input value. However, the data table results are a different matter. When you run the Data Table command, Excel enters an array formula in the interior of the data table. This formula is a `TABLE()` function (a special function available only by using the Data Table command) with the following syntax:

`{=TABLE(row_input_ref, column_input_ref)}`

Here, `row_input_ref` and `column_input_ref` are the cell references you entered in the Table dialog box. The braces (`{ }`) indicate that this is an array, which means that you can't change or delete individual elements of the array. If you want to change the results, you need to select the entire data table and then run the Data Table command again. If you just want to delete the results, you must first select the entire array and then delete it.

Creating a Two-Input Data Table

You also can set up data tables that take two input variables. For example, this would enable you to see the effect on an investment's future value when you enter two different values, such as the annual deposit and the interest rate.

1. Enter one set of values in a column below the formula.

2. Enter a second set of values to the right of the formula in the same row.

3. Select the range that includes the input values and the formula.

4. Select the Data tab.

5. Select What-If Analysis.

6. Select Data Table. Excel displays the Data Table dialog box.

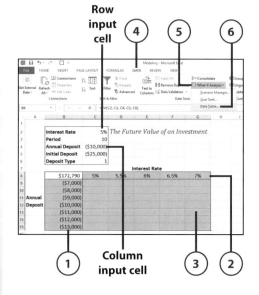

7. In the Row Input Cell text box, enter the cell address of the input cell that corresponds to the row values you entered.

8. In the Column Input Cell text box, enter the cell address of the input cell you want to use for the column values.

9. Select OK.

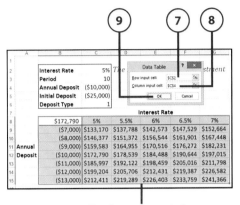

Excel runs through the various input combinations and then displays the results in the data table.

It's Not All Good

SLOW DATA TABLES

If you make changes to any of the variables in a table formula, Excel recalculates the entire table. This isn't a problem in small tables, but large ones can take a very long time to calculate. If you prefer to control the table recalculation, select Formulas, Calculation Options, Automatic Except for Data Tables. This tells Excel not to include data tables when it recalculates a worksheet. To recalculate your data tables, select Formulas, Calculate Now; to recalculate just the data tables in the current worksheet, select Formulas, Calculate Sheet.

Finding Solutions with Goal Seek

Here's a what-if question for you: What if you already know the result you want? For example, you might know that you want to have $50,000 saved to purchase new equipment five years from now, or that you have to achieve a 30% gross margin in your next budget. If you need to manipulate only a single variable to achieve these results, you can use Excel's Goal Seek feature. You tell Goal Seek the final value you need and which variable to change, and it finds a solution for you (if one exists).

When you set up a worksheet to use Goal Seek, you usually have a formula in one cell and the formula's variable—with an initial value—in another.

(Your formula can have multiple variables, but Goal Seek enables you to manipulate only one variable at a time.) Goal Seek operates by using an *iterative method* to find a solution. That is, Goal Seek first tries the variable's initial value to see whether that produces the result you want. If it doesn't, Goal Seek tries different values until it converges on a solution.

Before you run Goal Seek, you need to set up your worksheet in a particular way. This means doing three things:

1. Set up one cell as the *changing cell*. This is the value that Goal Seek will iteratively manipulate to attempt to reach the goal. Enter an initial value (such as 0) into the cell.

2. Set up the other input values for the formula and give them proper initial values.

3. Create a formula for Goal Seek to use to try to reach the goal.

Running Goal Seek

Goal Seek is useful for figuring out problems such as determining how much to set aside each year to end up with a $50,000 equipment fund in five years.

1. Select the Data tab.

2. Select What-If Analysis.

3. Select Goal Seek. Excel displays the Goal Seek dialog box.

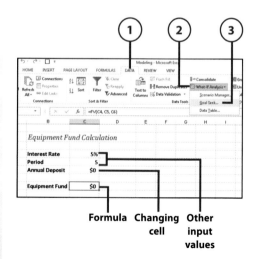

Formula   Changing   Other
          cell   input
                     values

4. Use the Set Cell text box to enter a reference to the cell that contains the formula you want Goal Seek to manipulate.

5. Use the To Value text box to enter the final value you want for the goal cell (such as 50000).

6. Use the By Changing Cell text box to enter a reference to the changing cell.

7. Click OK. Excel begins the iteration and displays the Goal Seek Status dialog box. When finished, the dialog box tells you whether Goal Seek found a solution.

8. If Goal Seek found a solution, you can accept the solution by clicking OK. To ignore the solution, click Cancel.

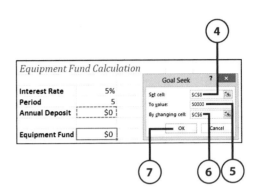

Pausing Goal Seek

Most of the time, Goal Seek finds a solution relatively quickly, and the Goal Seek Status dialog box appears on the screen for just a second or two. For longer operations, you can click Pause in the Goal Seek Status dialog box to stop Goal Seek. To walk through the process one iteration at a time, click Step. To resume Goal Seek, click Continue.

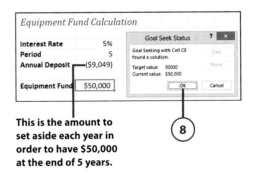

This is the amount to set aside each year in order to have $50,000 at the end of 5 years.

Creating Worksheet Scenarios

By definition, what-if analysis is not an exact science. All what-if models make guesses and assumptions based on history, expected events, or whatever voodoo comes to mind. A particular set of guesses and assumptions that you plug into a model is called a *scenario*. Because most what-if worksheets can take a wide range of input values, you usually end up with a large number of scenarios to examine. Instead of going through the tedious chore of inserting all these values into the appropriate cells, Excel has a Scenario Manager feature that can handle the process for you. This section shows you how to wield this useful tool.

As you've seen in this chapter, Excel has powerful features that enable you to build sophisticated models that can answer complex questions. The problem, though, isn't in *answering* questions, but in *asking* them. For example, suppose you have a worksheet model that analyzes a mortgage. You use this model to decide how much of a down payment to make, how long the term should be, and whether to include an extra principal paydown every month. Here are some possible questions to ask this model:

- How much will I save over the term of the mortgage if I use a shorter term, make a larger down payment, and include a monthly paydown?

- How much more will I end up paying if I extend the term, reduce the down payment, and forego the paydown?

These are examples of *scenarios* that you would plug into the appropriate cells in the model. Excel's Scenario Manager helps by letting you define a scenario separately from the worksheet. You can save specific values for any or all of the model's input cells, give the scenario a name, and then recall the name (and all the input values it contains) from a list.

Before creating a scenario, you need to decide which cells in your model will be the input cells. These will be the worksheet variables—the cells that, when you change them, change the results of the model. (Not surprisingly, Excel calls these the *changing cells*.) You can have as many as 32 changing cells in a scenario. For best results, follow these guidelines when setting up your worksheet for scenarios:

- The changing cells should be constants. Formulas can be affected by other cells, and that can throw off the entire scenario.

- To make it easier to set up each scenario, and to make your worksheet easier to understand, group the changing cells and label them.

- For even greater clarity, assign a range name to each changing cell.

Defining a Scenario

When your worksheet is set up the way you want it, you can use Excel's Scenario Manager tool to add a scenario to the sheet.

1. Select the Data tab.

2. Select What-If Analysis.

3. Select Scenario Manager. Excel displays the Scenario Manager dialog box.

4. Select Add. The Add Scenario dialog box opens.

5. Use the Scenario Name text box to enter a name for the scenario.

6. Use the Changing Cells text box to enter references to your worksheet's changing cells. You can type in the references (be sure to separate nonadjacent cells with commas) or select the cells directly on the worksheet.

7. Use the Comment text box to enter a description for the scenario. This description appears in the Comment section of the Scenario Manager dialog box.

8. Select OK. Excel displays the Scenario Values dialog box, which you use to enter the values you want to apply to the scenario's changing cells.

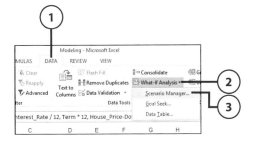

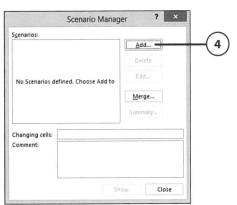

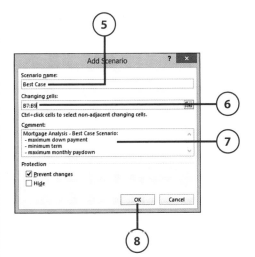

9. Use the text boxes to enter values for the changing cells.

Named Changing Cells

The Scenario Values dialog box displays the range name for each changing cell, which makes it easier to enter your numbers correctly. If your changing cells aren't named, Excel just displays the cell addresses instead.

10. To add more scenarios, select Add to return to the Add Scenario dialog box and repeat steps 5 through 9.

11. When you're done, select OK to return to the Scenario Manager dialog box.

12. Select Close to return to the worksheet.

Range names for the changing cells

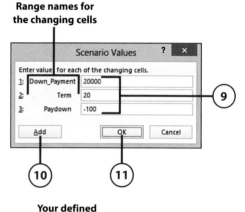

Your defined scenarios appear here.

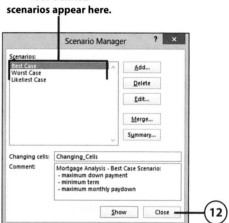

EDITING A SCENARIO

You can make changes to a scenario, whether you need to change the scenario's name, select different changing cells, or enter new values. Open the Scenario Manager and use the Scenarios list to select the scenario you want to edit. Select Edit to open the Edit Scenario dialog box, make your changes, if necessary, and click OK. In the Scenario Values dialog box, enter the new values, if necessary, and then select OK to return to the Scenario Manager dialog box.

Displaying a Scenario

After you define a scenario, you can enter its values into the changing cells by displaying the scenario from the Scenario Manager dialog box.

1. Select the Data tab.

2. Select What-If Analysis.

3. Select Scenario Manager. Excel displays the Scenario Manager dialog box.

4. In the Scenarios list, select the scenario you want to display.

5. Select Show. Excel enters the scenario values into the changing cells. Repeat steps 4 and 5 to display other scenarios.

6. Select Close to return to the worksheet.

When you select Show, Excel enters the values for the selected scenario into the changing cells.

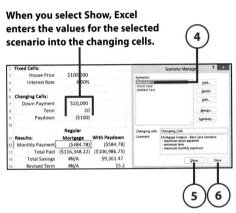

EASIER ACCESS TO SCENARIOS

Displaying a scenario isn't hard, but it does require having the Scenario Manager onscreen. You can bypass the Scenario Manager by adding the Scenario list to the Quick Access Toolbar. Pull down the Customize Quick Access Toolbar menu and then click More Commands. In the Select Commands From list, click All Commands. In the list of commands, click Scenario, click Add, and then click OK. (One caveat, though: If you select the same scenario twice in succession, Excel asks whether you want to redefine the scenario. Be sure to click No to keep the current scenario definition.)

Finding Optimum Solutions with Solver

Earlier you learned how to use Goal Seek to find solutions to formulas by changing a single variable. Unfortunately, many problems aren't so easy. You'll often face formulas with at least two and sometimes dozens of variables. Often, a problem will have more than one solution, and your challenge will be to find the *optimal* solution (that is, the one that maximizes profit, or minimizes costs, or matches other criteria). For these bigger challenges, you need a more muscular tool. Excel has just the answer: Solver. Solver is a sophisticated optimization program that enables you to find the solutions to complex problems that would otherwise require high-level mathematical analysis.

Solver is a powerful tool that most Excel users don't need. It would be overkill, for example, to use Solver to compute net profit given fixed revenue and cost figures. Many problems, however, require nothing less than the Solver approach. These problems cover many different fields and situations, but they all have the following characteristics in common:

- They have a single *objective cell* (also called the *target cell*) that contains a formula you want to maximize, minimize, or set to a specific value. This formula could be a calculation, such as total transportation expenses or net profit.

- The objective cell formula contains references to one or more *variable cells* (also called *unknowns* or *changing cells*). Solver adjusts these cells to find the optimal solution for the objective cell formula. These variable cells might include items such as units sold, shipping costs, or advertising expenses.

- Optionally, there are one or more *constraint cells* that must satisfy certain criteria. For example, you might require that advertising be less than 10% of total expenses, or that the discount to customers be a number between 40% and 60%.

Activating Solver

Solver is an add-in to Microsoft Excel, so you need to load Solver before you can use it.

1. Select File.

2. Select Options to open the Excel Options dialog box.

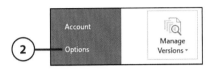

3. Select Add-Ins.

4. In the Manage list, select Excel Add-Ins.

5. Select Go. Excel displays the Add-Ins dialog box.

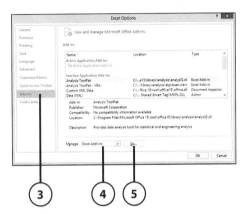

6. Select the Solver Add-In check box.

7. Select OK. Excel installs the add-in and adds a Solver button to the Data tab's Analysis group.

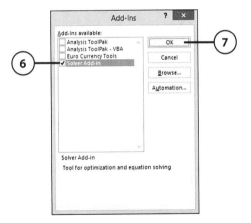

Running Solver

To help you get a feel for how Solver works, let's look at an example: computing the break-even point for two new products. (The break-even point is the number of units that need to be sold to produce a profit of 0.) The goal is to compute the number of units to sell for both products so that the total profit is 0.

1. Select the Data tab.

2. Select Solver. Excel displays the Solver Parameters dialog box.

3. In the Set Objective text box, enter a reference to the objective cell—that is, the cell with the formula you want to optimize.

4. In the To section, select the appropriate option button: Click Max to maximize the objective cell, click Min to minimize it, or click Value Of to solve for a particular value (in which case, you also need to enter the value in the text box provided). For a break-even problem, you'd select Value Of and enter 0 in the text box.

5. Use the By Changing Variable Cells text box to enter the cells you want Solver to change while it looks for a solution.

Maximum Variable Cells

You can enter a maximum of 200 cells in the By Changing Variable Cells text box.

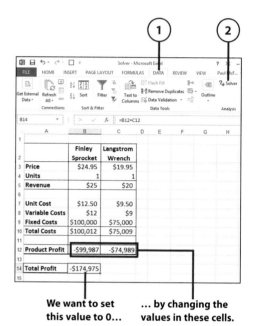

We want to set this value to 0... ... by changing the values in these cells.

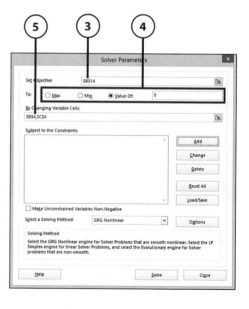

6. To add a constraint (that is, a condition that the solution must satisfy), select Add. Excel displays the Add Constraint dialog box.

7. In the Cell Reference text box, enter the cell you want to constrain.

8. Use the drop-down list in the middle of the dialog box to select the operator you want to use. The list contains several comparison operators for the constraint—less than or equal to (<=), equal to (=), and greater than or equal to (>=)—as well as two other data type operators—integer (int) and binary (bin). For the example, select the equal to operator (=).

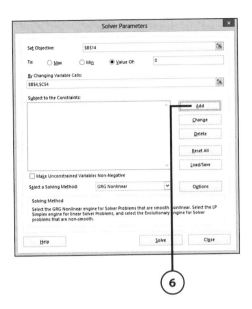

Understanding Constraint Operators

Use the int (integer) operator when you need a constraint, such as total employees, to be an integer value instead of a real number. Use the bin (binary) operator when you have a constraint that must be either TRUE or FALSE (or 1 or 0).

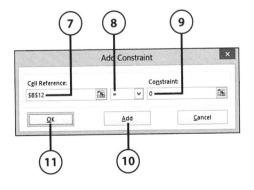

9. If you chose a comparison operator in step 8, use the Constraint text box to enter the value by which you want to restrict the cell.

10. If you want to enter more constraints, select Add and repeat steps 7 through 9.

11. When you're done, select OK to return to the Solver Parameters dialog box.

Maximum Constraints

You can add a maximum of 100 constraints.

12. Select Solve.

13. If you see the Show Trial Solution dialog box, select Continue. Repeat as needed. Finally, Solver displays the Solver Results dialog box, which tells you whether it found a solution.

14. If Solver found a solution that you want to use, select the Keep Solver Solution option and then select OK.

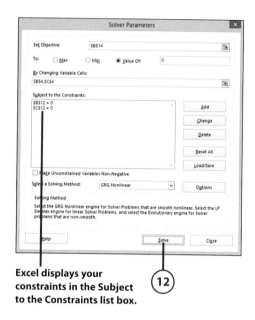

Excel displays your constraints in the Subject to the Constraints list box. ⑫

⑬

The constraints are met. ⑭

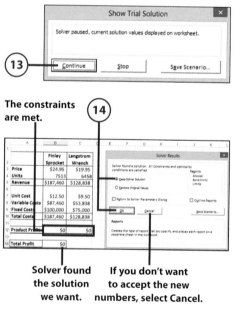

Solver found the solution we want.

If you don't want to accept the new numbers, select Cancel.

SAVING A SOLUTION AS A SCENARIO

>>>Go Further

If Solver finds a solution, you can save the variable cells as a scenario that you can display at any time. In the Solver Results dialog box, select Save Scenario to open the Save Scenario dialog box. Use the Scenario Name text box to enter a name for the scenario and then select OK. Excel returns you to the Solver Results dialog box, where you can keep or discard the solution, as appropriate.

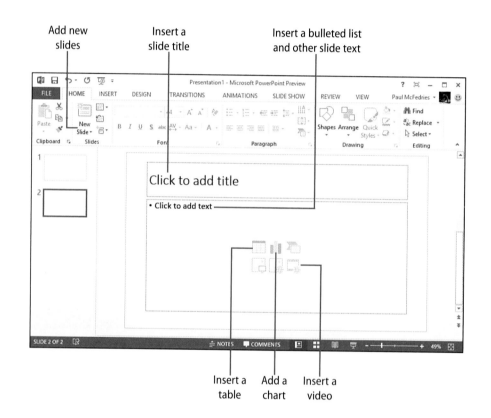

Add new slides

Insert a slide title

Insert a bulleted list and other slide text

Insert a table

Add a chart

Insert a video

In this chapter, you'll learn the basics of building a PowerPoint presentation, from inserting slides to adding text, graphics, charts, and other content.

→ Inserting and duplicating slides

→ Adding slide content, such as text, graphics, charts, and tables

→ Working with slide layouts

→ Adding presentation notes to a slide

→ Understanding and using the Slide Master

Building a PowerPoint Presentation

It's probably not a stretch to claim that, in terms of market share, PowerPoint is the most dominant software program in the world. A few years ago, Microsoft said that PowerPoint had 95% of the presentation graphics market, but it wouldn't surprise me if that number were even higher today. And with many of our kids learning and using PowerPoint in school, this dominance is poised to continue into the foreseeable future. In short, we live in a PowerPoint world.

So learning how to get along in this world is important, and this is what the next two chapters can help you do. The focus is on a PowerPoint "middle way" that avoids the two most common PowerPoint faults: drab, lifeless presentations that are ineffective because they bore the audience to tears, and *PowerPointlessness*— those overly fancy formats, transitions, sounds, and other effects that have no discernible purpose, use, or benefit. With the middle way, you learn how to create attractive presentations that offer visual interest without sacrificing clarity.

Adding a Slide to the Presentation

The heart and soul of any presentation is the collection of slides that comprise the bulk of its content and that serve as both the focal point and the organizing structure of the talk. The slides are the bridge between the audience—who, for the most part, has no idea what you're going to talk about—and yourself—who knows exactly what you want to say (presumably!). Building an effective presentation consists mostly of creating and organizing slides, which in turn involves four things:

- The content—the text and graphics—presented on each slide

- The organization of the content presented on each slide

- The formatting applied to each slide: fonts, colors, background, and so on

- The placement of the slides within the context of the entire presentation

The bulk of this chapter takes you through various PowerPoint techniques that support these four design ideas.

Understanding Slide Layouts

Before we get to the specifics of adding a slide, you should understand that all slides contain some combination of the following three elements:

- **Title**—This is a text box that you normally use to add a title for the slide.

- **Text**—This is a text box that you normally use to add text to the slide, which is usually a collection of bullets.

- **Content**—This is a container into which you add any type of content supported by PowerPoint: text, a picture, or a SmartArt graphic. In some cases, PowerPoint displays placeholders for specific types of content. For example, a Picture placeholder can contain only a picture.

In each case, the new slide contains one or more *placeholders*, and your job is to fill in a placeholder with text or a content object. Each slide uses some combination of Title, Text, and Content placeholders, and the arrangement of these placeholders on a slide is called the *slide layout*. PowerPoint offers nine layouts:

- **Title Slide**—A slide with two text boxes: a larger one for the overall presentation title and a smaller one for the subtitle

- **Title and Content**—A slide with a Title placeholder and a Content placeholder

- **Section Header**—A slide with two Text placeholders: one for the description and one for the title of a new presentation section

- **Two Content**—A slide with a Title placeholder above two Content placeholders placed side by side

- **Comparison**—A slide with a Title placeholder, two Content placeholders placed side by side, and two Text placeholders (one above each Content placeholder)

- **Title Only**—A slide with just a Title placeholder

- **Blank**—A slide with no placeholders

- **Content with Caption**—A Content placeholder with two Text placeholders to the left of it: one for the content title and the other for the content description

- **Picture with Caption**—A Picture placeholder with two Text placeholders beneath it: one for the picture title and the other for the picture description

Inserting a New Slide

Inserting a new slide into your presentation is a straightforward matter of deciding what content you want on the slide and then deciding which slide layout would best display that content. Note that you can always change the slide layout later on (see "Changing the Layout of a Slide").

1. In the slide sorter, select the slide after which you want the new slide to appear.

2. Select the Home tab.

3. Select the bottom half of the New Slide button.

4. Select the slide layout you want to use. PowerPoint inserts the new slide.

Keyboard Shortcut

You can quickly add a slide that uses the Title and Content layout by pressing Ctrl+M.

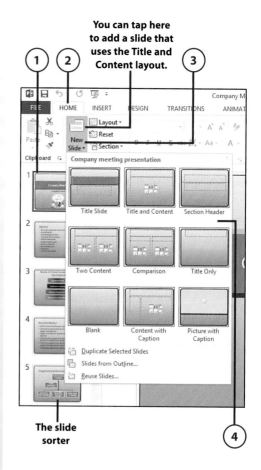

You can tap here to add a slide that uses the Title and Content layout.

The slide sorter

Duplicating a Slide

If you have a slide in the current presentation that has similar content and formatting to what you want for a new slide, you can save yourself a great deal of time by inserting a duplicate of that slide and then adjusting the copy as needed.

1. In the slide sorter, select the slide you want to duplicate.

2. Select the Home tab.

3. Select the bottom half of the New Slide button.

4. Select Duplicate Selected Slides. PowerPoint creates a copy of the slide and inserts the copy below the selected slide.

Duplicating Via Copy-and-Paste

A quicker way to duplicate a slide is to select it, select the Home tab, select Copy (or press Ctrl+C) to copy it, and then select Paste (or press Ctrl+V) to paste the copy. If you want the copy to appear in a particular place within the presentation, select the slide after which you want the copy to appear and then select Paste (or press Ctrl+V).

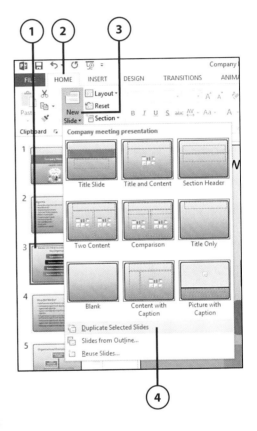

REUSING A SLIDE FROM ANOTHER PRESENTATION

One of the secrets of PowerPoint productivity is to avoid redoing work you have performed in the past. If you have a slide with boilerplate legal disclaimer text, why re-create it in each presentation? If you create an organization chart slide and your organization has not changed, you don't need to build the chart from scratch every time you want to add it to a presentation.

In this section, you saw how to duplicate a slide from the current presentation. However, the far more common scenario is that the slide you want to reuse exists in another presentation. Select the Home tab, select New Slide, and then select Reuse Slides to open the Reuse Slides task pane. If this is the first time you've displayed the Reuse Slides pane in the current PowerPoint session, select the Open a PowerPoint File link; otherwise, pull down the Browse list, select Browse File, select the presentation you want to use, and then select Open. PowerPoint adds the presentation's slides to the Reuse Slides task pane. If you want the formatting of the original slide to appear in the new slide, select the Keep Source Formatting check box to activate it. Select the slide you want to reuse to insert it into the presentation.

Adding Data to a Slide

After you have added one or more slides, the next step is to fill in the placeholders. The next few sections take you through some of the details. For now, you should know that the Content placeholder contains six icons grouped together in the middle of the box. These icons represent the six main types of content you can add to the placeholder, and clicking each icon launches the process of inserting that content type. In the sections that follow, I ignore the picture-related icons because I already covered adding graphics in Chapter 3, "Working with Office RT Graphics."

Adding Text

With a Title or Text placeholder, select inside the placeholder to enable editing and then type your text. In a Text placeholder, PowerPoint assumes that you'll be adding bullet points, so the Bullets format is on by default. PowerPoint supports four standard *list levels*, which determine where a bullet appears in the list hierarchy:

- **Level 1**—This is the main level. It uses a solid, round bullet and appears flush with the left side of the placeholder.

- **Level 2**—This is the next level in the hierarchy. It uses a slightly smaller bullet and appears indented by one tab stop from the left side of the placeholder.

- **Level 3**—This is the next level in the hierarchy. It uses an even smaller bullet and appears indented by two tab stops from the left side of the placeholder.

- **Level 4**—This is the final level in the hierarchy. It uses the smallest bullet and appears indented by three tab stops from the left side of the placeholder.

You can actually create higher and higher levels, but the bullet remains the same size and PowerPoint simply indents the bullets further from the left. The next section illustrates what these levels look like.

Creating a Bulleted List

Populating a Text placeholder with a bulleted list will likely be your most common PowerPoint chore.

1. Tap inside a Text placeholder to open it for editing. PowerPoint displays the first bullet.

2. Type the text for the list item.

3. Press Enter. PowerPoint adds a bullet for the next item in the list.

If you prefer to enter just regular text, select Home and then Bullets to turn off the bulleted list format.

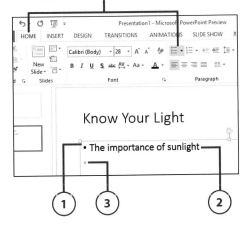

4. Repeat steps 2 and 3 to add more items to the list.

5. To increase the list level of the current item, select the Home tab and then select Increase List Level.

6. To decrease the list level of the current item, select the Home tab and then select Decrease List Level.

Keyboard Shortcut

To change the list level via the keyboard, place the insertion point at the beginning of an item and then press either Tab to increase the list level, or Shift+Tab to decrease the list level.

7. Repeat steps 2 to 6 until your list is complete.

8. Position the insertion point at the end of the last item and then press Enter twice to tell PowerPoint that your bulleted list is done.

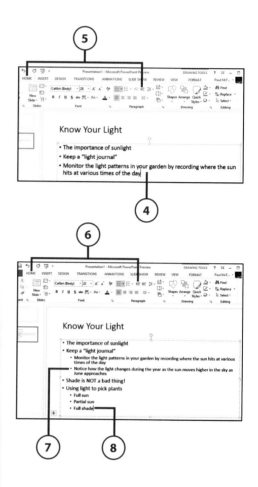

CONVERTING REGULAR TEXT TO A BULLETED LIST

What if a slide already includes regular text that you'd prefer to display as a bulleted list? Select the entire list, select the Home tab, and then select the Bullets icon in the Ribbon. PowerPoint converts the text into a bulleted list.

Adding a Video

Earlier in this chapter (see "Understanding Slide Layouts"), I described PowerPoint slide layouts and said you need a Content placeholder to insert a picture into a slide. Five layouts come with Content placeholders: Title and Content, Two Content, Comparison, Content with Caption, and Picture with Caption. Before you can insert a video into a presentation, you must first add a slide that uses one of these five layouts.

1. Select a slide that contains a Content placeholder.

2. In the Content placeholder, select the Insert Video icon. PowerPoint displays the Insert Video dialog box.

3. Select From a File. PowerPoint displays the Insert Video dialog box.

4. Select the location of the video.

5. Select the video file you want to insert.

6. Select Insert. PowerPoint inserts the video into the placeholder.

7. Drag the video's selection handles to set the size of the video.

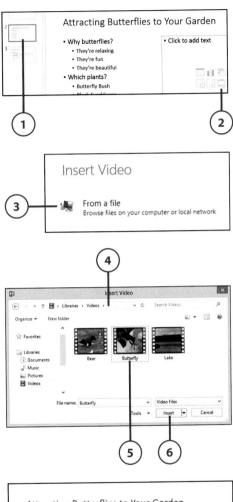

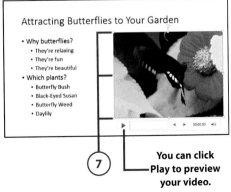

You can click Play to preview your video.

>>>Go Further

EMBEDDING AN ONLINE VIDEO

If you have an online video you'd prefer to use, you can insert a special code that embeds the video into your slide. All online video sites—including YouTube—offer with each video a special code called the *video embed code*, as well as a mechanism for copying that code. Once you've copied the embed code for the video you want, select a slide that contains a Content placeholder and then select the Insert Video icon to open the Insert Video dialog box. Tap inside the From a Video Embed Code text box, paste the copied code, and then tap the Insert arrow.

Adding a Chart

If you have numeric results to present, one surefire way to make your audience's eyes glaze over is show them a slide that is crammed with numbers. Most slide shows present the "big picture," and nothing translates numeric values into a digestible big-picture format better than a chart. PowerPoint uses Excel charts, which means that adding a chart to a PowerPoint slide is not that much different from creating a chart in Excel, which I explain in detail in Chapter 9, "Visualizing Excel Data with Charts."

1. Select a slide that contains a Content placeholder.

2. In the Content placeholder, select the Insert Chart icon. PowerPoint displays the Insert Chart dialog box.

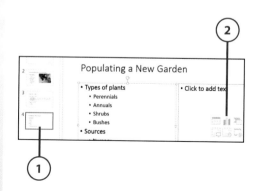

3. Select the chart type you want to use.

4. Select OK. PowerPoint launches Excel, adds sample data to a worksheet, inserts a chart into the slide, and splits the screen with both applications.

5. Adjust the worksheet labels and values as needed.

6. When you are done, select Close.

7. Tap the chart title and then type the title you want to use.

8. To change the chart data, select Design, Edit Data, Edit Data.

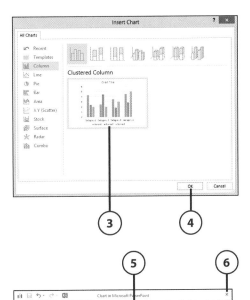

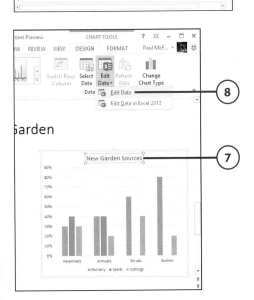

Adding a Table

If you want to present data that would look best in a row-and-column format, use a table. Note that a PowerPoint table is nearly identical to a Word table, so see the section "Building a Table" in Chapter 5, "Working with Page Layout in Word," for more table details.

1. Select a slide that contains a Content placeholder.

2. In the Content placeholder, select the Insert Table icon. PowerPoint displays the Insert Table dialog box.

3. Specify the number of columns you want in your table.

4. Specify the number of rows you want in your table.

5. Select OK. PowerPoint inserts the table into the slide.

6. Type your column headings.

7. Type your table data.

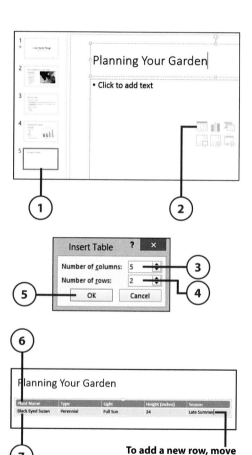

To add a new row, move the insertion point to the end of the last cell and then press Tab.

Working with Slides

Now that your presentation is populated with a few slides and your slides have some content on them, it's time to learn a few useful techniques for working with your slides. The rest of this chapter shows you how to select and rearrange slides, change the slide layout, hide a slide, add slide notes, and work with the Slide Master.

Selecting Slides

To work with slides, you must first select one or more. Here are the techniques you can use in the slide sorter:

- To select a single slide, tap it.

- To select multiple, consecutive slides, tap the first slide, hold down Shift, and then tap the last slide.

- To select multiple, nonconsecutive slides, tap the first slide, hold down Ctrl, and tap each of the other slides.

- To select all the slides, select any slide and then press Ctrl+A. You can also choose Home, Select, Select All.

Rearranging Slides

PowerPoint gives you two different methods for changing the order of slides in a presentation:

- In the slide sorter, select the slide you want to move, select the Home tab, and then select Cut (or press Ctrl+X). Select the slide after which you want the moved slide to appear, and then select Paste (or press Ctrl+V).

- In the slide sorter, tap and drag the slide and drop it below the slide after which you want it to appear.

Changing the Layout of a Slide

If the original layout you applied to a slide is not what you want, you can change it.

1. Select the slide or slides you want to change.

2. Select the Home tab.

3. Select Layout. PowerPoint displays a gallery of slide layouts.

4. Select the layout you want to use. PowerPoint applies the new layout to the selected slides.

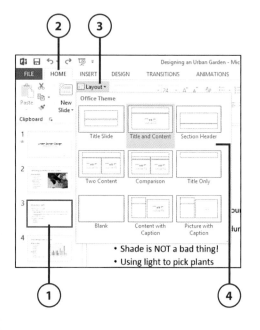

No Content Is Lost

It's okay to select a slide layout that has fewer placeholders than the current slide layout. In this case, Excel retains the data, but it now appears in the slide as a separate object rather than in its own placeholder.

Hiding a Slide

In some presentations, there may be slides you don't want to show:

- You might have a short version and a long version of a presentation.

- You might want to omit certain slides, depending on whether you are presenting to managers, salespeople, or engineers.

- You might have "internal" and "external" versions; that is, you might have one version for people who work at your company and a different version for people from outside the company.

You could accommodate these different scenarios by creating copies of a presentation and then removing slides as appropriate. However, this process takes a great deal of work, wastes disk space, and is inefficient when one slide changes and you have to make the same change in every version of the presentation that includes the slide.

A much better solution is to use a single presentation but mark the slides you don't want to show as *hidden*. PowerPoint skips hidden slides when you present the show.

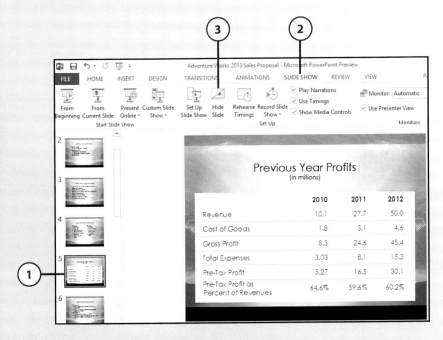

1. In the slide sorter, select the slide you want to hide.

2. Select the Slide Show tab.

3. Select Hide Slide. PowerPoint displays a faded version of the slide thumbnail and adds a strikethrough to the slide number.

Unhiding a Slide
To unhide a slide, select it, select Slide Show, and then select Hide Slide.

>>>Go Further

DELETING A SLIDE

If you have a slide that you no longer need, you should delete it from your presentation to reduce the size of the presentation, reduce clutter in the slide sorter, and prevent the slide from appearing when you present the show. To delete a slide, use the slide sorter to tap and hold the slide for a few seconds to display the Mini Toolbar, and then tap Delete.

Adding Notes to a Slide

When determining the content of a presentation, you keep the actual amount of information on a slide to a minimum—just the high-level points to provide the framework for the topics you want to present. How, then, do you keep track of the details you want to cover for each slide? You add notes to the presentation. When you run through the presentation in PowerPoint's Reading View mode, you (or any other viewer) can display the notes.

1. Select the slide you want to work with.

2. If you don't see the Notes page (the section with the Click to Add Notes text) below the slide, select the View tab and then select Notes.

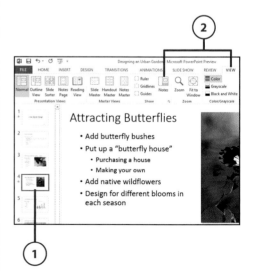

3. Tap anywhere inside the Notes page below the slide. PowerPoint converts the section to a text box.

4. Type your notes.

5. Tap outside the Notes page to close it for editing.

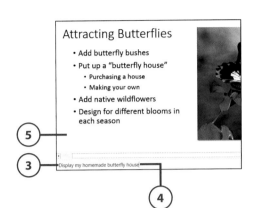

Making Room for Notes

If you want more room to type in the Notes page, PowerPoint provides a couple of choices. First, you can tap and drag the separator bar at the top of the Notes page. Drag the bar up until the Notes page is the size you want, and then release the bar. This gives you less room for the slide, but you can also return the Notes page to its original size after you have added your notes. The second way to get a larger Notes area is to select the View tab and then select Notes Page. This changes the view to display the full Notes Page text box.

USING SLIDE NOTES

Here are some suggested ways you can use notes:

- As additional details for the audience.

- As a student guide. If you use a presentation as your primary teaching medium, you can put additional information on notes pages for your learners.

- As an instructor's guide. Again, if you teach from your presentation, you might have points you want to make, or other information associated with a particular slide. Add this information as notes, and you have your instructor's guide, perfectly in sync with the information you're giving your learners.

- As your presentation notes.

- As additional detailed handouts for your audience.

The first two points here apply to both offline presentations (where you present in front of an audience) and online presentations (where audience members run the show themselves), but the last three apply only to offline presentations.

Understanding the Slide Master

One of PowerPoint's templates might be just right for your presentation. If so, great! Your presentation's design will be one less thing to worry about on your way to an effective presentation. Often, however, a template is just right except for the background color, title alignment, or font. Or perhaps you need the company's logo to appear on each slide. Using the template as a starting point, you can make changes to the overall presentation so that it's just right for your needs.

However, what if your presentation already has a number of slides? It will probably require a great deal of work to change the background, alignment, or font on every slide. Fortunately, PowerPoint offers a much easier way: the Slide Master, which is available for every presentation. The Slide Master acts as a kind of "design center" for your presentation. The Slide Master's typefaces, type sizes, bullet styles, colors, alignment options, line spacing, and more are used on each slide in your presentation. Not only that, but any object you add to the Slide Master—a piece of clip art, a company logo, and so on—also appears in the same position on each slide.

The beauty of the Slide Master is that any change you make to this one slide, PowerPoint propagates to all the slides in your presentation. Need to change the background color? Just change the background color of the Slide Master. Prefer a different type size for top-level items? Change the type size for the top-level item shown on the Slide Master. You can also make separate adjustments to the masters of the seven standard layouts (Title Slide, Title and Content, and so on).

Working with the Slide Master

Before you can work with the Slide Master, you must first switch to it.

1. Select the View tab.

2. Select Slide Master. PowerPoint switches to Slide Master view.

3. Select the Slide Master and then make your changes to the Slide Master formatting.

Formatting the Slide Master

Whether you're working with the Slide Master or a layout master, you can format the text, background, bullets, and colors as if you were working in a regular slide.

4. To apply a theme to the masters, select Slide Master, Themes and then select a theme.

5. Select the layout master you want to work with.

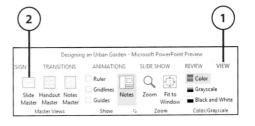

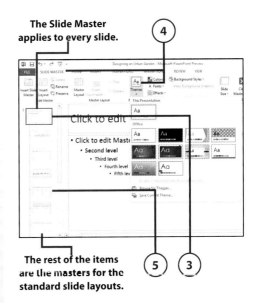

The Slide Master applies to every slide.

The rest of the items are the masters for the standard slide layouts.

6. Select a placeholder.

7. To size a placeholder, tap and drag the selection handles.

8. To move a placeholder, tap and drag the placeholder border (being careful to not drag a selection handle).

9. To add a placeholder to the layout master, select Slide Master, Insert Placeholder, and then select the placeholder type you want.

10. To toggle the title on and off for the layout master, select the Title check box.

11. To display an object—such as clip art or a text box—on the layout, select the Insert tab and then insert the object into the master.

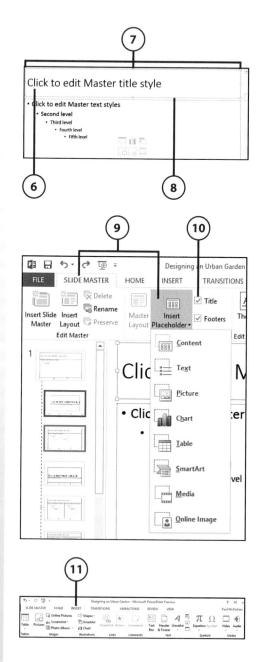

>>>Go Further

ADDING A CUSTOM LAYOUT

To add a custom layout to the Slide Master, select the Slide Master tab and then select Insert Layout. To supply a name to the new custom layout, select it, select Slide Master, Rename, then use the Rename Layout dialog box to type a new name, and select Rename. Use the Slide Master, Insert Placeholder command to add placeholders to the new layout.

12. Select the Slide Master tab.

13. Select Close Master View.

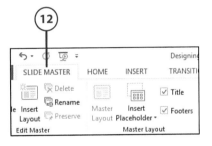

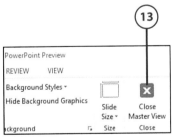

Start the
slide show

Add transitions
between slides

Animate slide
objects

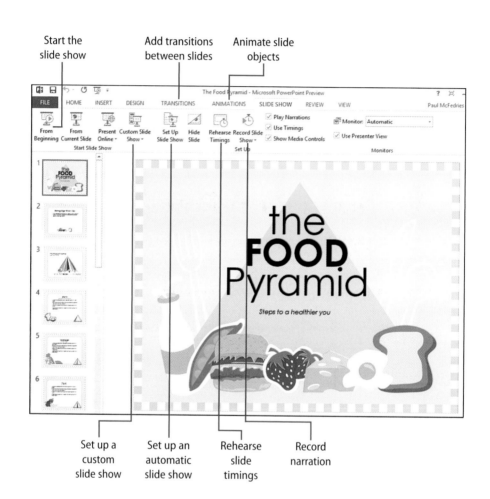

Set up a
custom
slide show

Set up an
automatic
slide show

Rehearse
slide
timings

Record
narration

In this chapter, you'll learn how to work with PowerPoint slide shows, including how to set up slide animations, work out slide timings, record narration, and run the slide show.

→ Adding transitions to your slides

→ Working with predefined and custom animations

→ Rehearsing the timing of each slide

→ Recording narration for a slide or entire presentation

→ Starting and navigating a slide show

Working with PowerPoint Slide Shows

In Chapter 11, "Building a PowerPoint Presentation," I mentioned that your goal when creating your slides should be to achieve a balance between eye candy and content. That is, although you need to tweak your slide fonts, colors, and effects to a certain extent to add visual interest, you do not want to go so far that your message is lost.

The same idea applies to the slide show as a whole, particularly if you want to add some dynamism to the presentation with slide transitions and object animations. These are fine additions to any presentation, but going overboard and therefore overwhelming your content is easy to do. This chapter gives you the details and techniques that can help you create the dynamic and interesting slide shows that audiences crave, but always remember that the message is the most important thing in any presentation.

Defining Slide Animations

Many years ago, someone defined *fritterware* as any software program that offered so many options and settings that you could fritter away hours at a time tweaking and playing with the program. PowerPoint's animation features certainly put it into the fritterware category because whiling away entire afternoons playing with transitions, entrance effects, motion paths, and other animation features is not hard. So consider yourself warned that the information in the next few sections might have adverse effects on your productivity.

Animation Guidelines

Before you learn how to apply slide transitions and object animations, it's worth taking a bit of time now to run through a few guidelines for making the best use of slide show animations:

- **Enhance your content**—The goal of any animation should always be to enhance your presentation, either to emphasize a slide object or to keep up your audience's interest. Resist the temptation to add effects just because you think they are cool or fun, because chances are most of your audience won't see them that way.

- **Remember that transitions can be useful**—Using some sort of effect to transition from one slide to the next is a good idea because it adds visual interest, gives the audience a short breather, and helps you control the pacing of your presentation.

- **Remember that transitions can be distracting**—A slide transition is only as useful as it is unremarkable. If everybody leaves your presentation thinking "Nice transitions!", then you have a problem because they *should* be thinking about your message. Simple transitions such as fades, wipes, and dissolves add interest but do not get in the way. On the other hand, if you have objects flying in from all corners of the screen, your content will seem like a letdown.

- **When it comes to transitions and animations, variety is *not* the spice of life**—Avoid the temptation to use many different transitions and animations in a single presentation. Just as slide text looks awful if you use too many fonts, your presentations will look amateurish if you use too many animated effects.

- **Keep up the pace**—For transitions, keep the duration setting low to ensure that the transition from one slide to another never takes more than a few seconds. Also, avoid running multiple object animations at the same time because it can take an awfully long time for the effect to finish, and audiences *never* like having their time wasted on such things.

- **Match your animations to your audience**—If you are presenting to sales and marketing types, your entire presentation will be a bit on the flashy side, so you can probably get away with more elaborate animations; in a no-nonsense presentation to board members, animations and transitions should be as simple as possible.

Setting Up a Slide Transition

A *slide transition* is a special effect that displays the next slide in the presentation. For example, in a *fade* transition, the next slide gradually materializes, while in a *blinds* transition the next slide appears with an effect similar to opening Venetian blinds. PowerPoint has nearly 40 different slide transitions, and for each one you can control the transition speed, the sound effect that goes along with the transition, and the trigger for the transition (a tap or a time interval).

1. Select the slide you want to work with. If you want to apply the transition to multiple slides, select the slides.

2. Select the Transitions tab.

3. Select the More button in the Transition to This Slide group. PowerPoint displays a gallery of transitions.

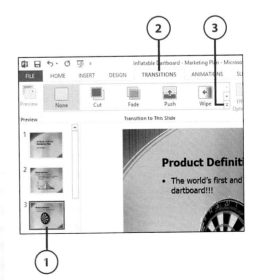

4. Select the transition effect you want. PowerPoint previews the transition.

5. If the transition effect comes with any options, select Effect Options to see what's available.

6. In the Sound list, select the sound that you want to play during the transition. (If you are not sure which one you want, you can hover the mouse pointer over any sound effect to hear it played.)

7. Use the Duration spin box to set the time, in seconds, that it takes to play the transition.

8. If you want to move to the next slide by tapping the screen during the slide show, leave the On Mouse Click check box selected.

9. If you want to move to the next slide automatically after a set number of minutes and/or seconds, select the After check box and then specify the time interval.

10. Select Preview to try out your transition.

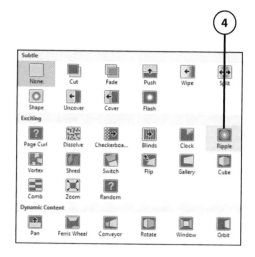

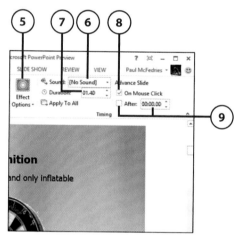

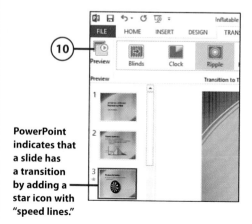

PowerPoint indicates that a slide has a transition by adding a star icon with "speed lines."

SPECIAL "SOUNDS"

The Sound list contains four special cases:

- **[No Sound]**—Select this item to run the transition without a sound effect.

- **[Stop Previous Sound]**—If the previous slide transition used a long-running sound effect, select this item to stop that sound.

- **Other Sound**—Select this item to display the Add Audio dialog box. Select the sound file you want to use and then select OK.

- **Loop Until Next Sound**—Select this command to repeat the chosen sound effect until the next effect begins.

There are very few circumstances where the Loop Until Next Sound option is appropriate, so exercise some caution with this command. Unless your looped sound is a pleasant snippet of music (that loops smoothly) or an effect that requires some time—such as a ticking clock—the constant noise will just distract or annoy your audience.

Animating Slide Objects

A dynamic presentation is one where the slide text, graphics, and other objects are not static and lifeless on the screen. Instead, such a presentation takes advantage of PowerPoint's four types of animation effects:

- **Entrance**—These effects control how the object comes onto the slide.

- **Emphasis**—These effects add emphasis to an object by altering various text properties, including the typeface, size, boldface, italic, and color.

- **Exit**—These effects control how the object goes off the slide when you move to the next slide.

- **Motion Paths**—These effects control the path that the object follows when it comes onto and goes off the slide.

Again, you don't want to overdo any of these effects, but neither should you ignore them.

Adding an Animation

PowerPoint's Ribbon offers the Animations tab, which makes it easy to select an animation for any object on a slide.

1. Select the slide you want to work with.

2. Select the slide object you want to animate.

Applying Animation

You can apply animation to any object, including the title and text placeholders, individual bullets or paragraphs (select the bullet or paragraph text), and drawing layer objects such as text boxes, shapes, clip art, pictures, SmartArt, charts, and tables.

3. Select the Animations tab.

4. Select the More button in the Animation group. PowerPoint displays the Animation gallery.

5. Select the animation you want to apply to the object. PowerPoint previews the animation.

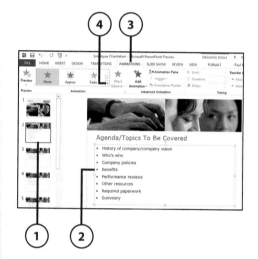

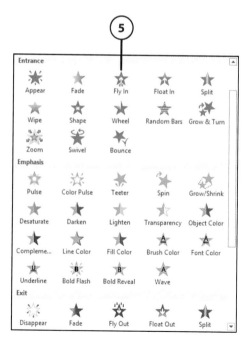

6. If the animation effect comes with any options, select Effect Options to see what's available.

7. Use the Start list to determine when the animation begins. On Click means it begins when you click the screen, which is usually what you want. You can also select With Previous to have the animation run at the same time as the previous animation, or After Previous to have the animation run immediately after the previous animation is complete.

8. Use the Duration spin box to set the time, in seconds, that it takes to play the transition.

9. Use the Delay spin box to set the time, in seconds, that PowerPoint waits before starting the transition.

10. To change the order in which the animations occur, click the object and then use the Move Earlier and Move Later commands to move the object up or down in the animation order.

11. Select Preview to try out your animation.

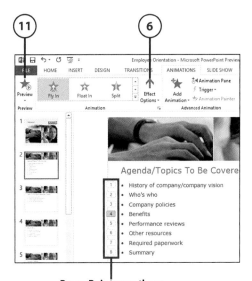

PowerPoint uses these
numbers to indicate
the order in which the
slide animations occur.

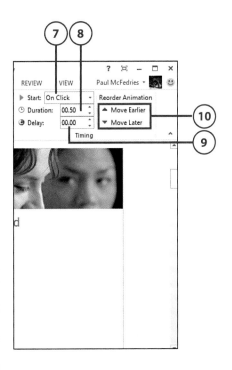

MAKING BULLETS APPEAR ONE AT A TIME

One of the most popular animation effects is making bullets appear individually, usually in response to a mouse click. This very useful presentation trick gives you full control over the display of your bullets. By animating bullets individually, you can prevent your audience from being distracted by bullets beyond the one you're currently discussing; you can hide bullets that contain "surprise" results until you're ready to present them; you can place extra emphasis on the individual bullets because they don't enter the slide individually as a group; and you add pizzazz by giving each bullet a different animation effect. (Although, of course, you want to be careful here that you don't induce animation overload on your audience.) If you've applied an animation to a text placeholder that contains bullets, you can make the bullets appear one at a time by selecting Effect Options and then selecting By Paragraph.

Preparing a Slide Show

Once you have your slides set up with content, transitions, and animations, you're ready to start thinking about the slide show that you'll be presenting. There isn't a ton that you have to do to prepare for the slide show, but there are a few tasks you should consider. These include rehearsing the timings of each slide, adding narration to individual slides or even the entire presentation, and putting together a custom slide show. The next few sections provide the details.

PowerPoint has a feature that can greatly improve your presentations. The feature is called Rehearse Timings and the idea behind it is simple: You run through ("rehearse") your presentation, and while you do this, PowerPoint keeps track of the amount of time you spend on each slide. This is useful for two reasons:

- If you have only so much time to present the slide show, Rehearse Timings lets you know if your overall presentation runs too long or too short.

- After the rehearsal, you can examine the time spent on each slide. If you have consecutive slides where you spend a short amount of time on each, consider consolidating two or more of the slides into a single slide. Conversely, if you have some slides where you spend a great deal of time, consider splitting each one into two or more slides to avoid overwhelming (or boring) your audience.

PowerPoint also gives you a third reason to use Rehearse Timings: You can save the resulting timings and use them to run a slide show automatically. You find out how to do this later in this chapter (see "Setting Up an Automatic Slide Show").

Rehearsing Slide Timings

Before getting started, open the presentation you want to rehearse and collect any notes or props you'll use during the presentation.

1. Select the Slide Show tab.

2. Select Rehearse Timings. PowerPoint starts the slide show and displays the Rehearsal toolbar.

3. Present the slide exactly as you would during the actual presentation.

Resetting and Pausing

If you mess up a slide, you can start the timing of that slide over again by selecting the Repeat button. If you just need a second or two to gather your thoughts, select Pause, instead.

---

4. Select Next to move on to the next slide.

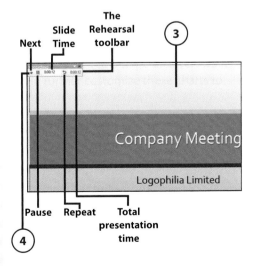

5. Repeat steps 3 and 4 for the entire presentation. When the presentation is done, PowerPoint displays the total presentation time and asks whether you want to save the slide timings.

6. To save the timings, select Yes; otherwise, select No.

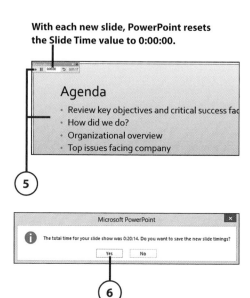

With each new slide, PowerPoint resets the Slide Time value to 0:00:00.

Recording Narration

Part of the appeal of a good presentation is that it feels like we are being told a story. Some words or images appear on a screen, but a person presents the underlying narrative for those words and images. There is something about a live human voice explicating some idea or process that is appealing on a deep level.

However, times may occur when you require a recorded voice for some or all of a presentation:

- You might have a slide that consists of a recorded greeting from the CEO or someone else at your company.

- You might have several slides where an expert does the presenting. If that person cannot be at your presentation, you need to record his or her material.

- You might be setting up an automatic presentation and so require recorded narration for the entire show.

PowerPoint can handle all of these situations by enabling you to record narration from one or more slides or for the entire presentation.

Recording Narration for a Slide

If needed, you can record narration for just a single slide.

1. Select the slide you want to narrate.

2. Select the Slide Show tab.

3. Select the bottom half of the Record Slide Show button.

4. Select Start Recording from Current Slide. PowerPoint displays the Record Slide Show dialog box.

5. If you have already rehearsed the slide timings, you can deselect the Slide and Animation Timings check box.

6. Make sure the Narration and Laser Pointer check box is selected.

7. Select the Start Recording button. PowerPoint displays the slide and the Rehearsal toolbar.

8. Run through your narration.

9. When you're done, select More.

10. Select End Show. PowerPoint adds a sound icon to the slide.

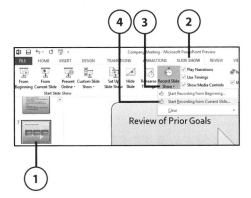

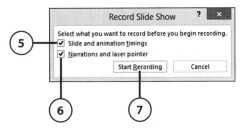

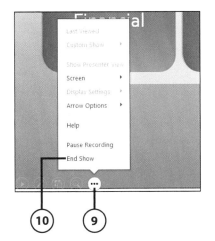

11. Select the sound icon.

12. Select the Playback tab.

13. Use the Start list to select when the narration starts: Automatically (the narration begins when you display the slide) or On Click (the narration begins when you click the slide).

Clearing the Narration

If you're not happy with your narration, you can remove it from the slide. Select the slide you used for the narration, select the Slide Show tab, select the bottom half of the Record Slide Show button, select Clear, and then select Clear Narration on Current Slide.

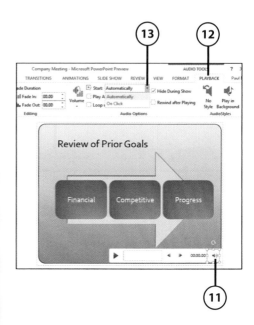

Recording Narration for an Entire Presentation

If you need to record narration for the entire presentation, collect your notes, pull up your microphone, and then follow these steps.

1. Select the Slide Show tab.

2. Select the bottom half of the Record Slide Show button.

3. Select Start Recording from Beginning. PowerPoint displays the Record Slide Show dialog box.

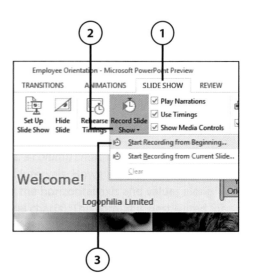

4. If you have already rehearsed the slide timings, you can deselect the Slide and Animation Timings check box.

5. Make sure the Narration and Laser Pointer check box is selected.

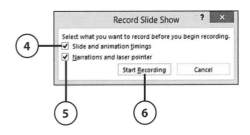

6. Select the Start Recording button. PowerPoint opens the first slide and displays the Rehearsal toolbar.

7. Present the slide exactly as you would during the actual presentation, including your narration.

8. Select Next to display the next slide.

9. Repeat steps 3 and 4 until the presentation is done. PowerPoint adds a sound icon to each slide in the presentation.

10. For each slide, select the sound icon.

11. Select the Playback tab.

12. Use the Start list to select when the narration starts: Automatically (the narration begins when you display the slide) or On Click (the narration begins when you click the slide).

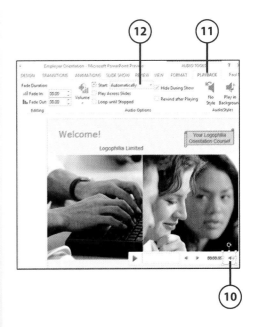

Running the Show Without Narration

If you need to run the slide show without narration, select the Slide Show tab and then select Set Up Slide Show to display the Set Up Show dialog box. Select the Show Without Narration check box and then select OK.

Clearing the Entire Narration

If you're not happy with any of your narration, you can remove it from the presentation. Select the slide you used for the narration, select the Slide Show tab, select the bottom half of the Record Slide Show button, select Clear, and then select Clear Narration on All Slides.

Setting Up Multiple Versions of a Slide Show

Having two or more versions of a presentation is common. Here are some examples:

- You might have a short version and a long version of a presentation.

- You might want to omit certain slides depending on whether you are presenting to managers, salespeople, or engineers.

- You might have "internal" and "external" versions; that is, you might have one version for people who work at your company and a different version for people from outside the company.

You could accommodate these different scenarios by creating copies of the presentation and then removing or reordering the slides as appropriate. However, this process takes a great deal of work, wastes disk space, and is inefficient when one slide changes and you have to make the same change in every version of the presentation that includes the slide.

A much better solution is to define one or more custom slide shows, which is a customized list of slides and the order in which you want them to appear.

Creating a Custom Slide Show

You create a custom slide show by deciding which slides you want to appear in the presentation and then positioning those slides in the order you prefer.

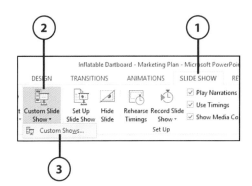

1. Select the Slide Show tab.

2. Select Custom Slide Show.

3. Select Custom Shows. PowerPoint displays the Custom Shows dialog box.

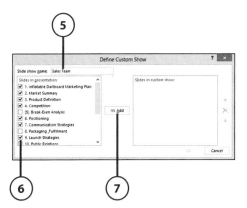

4. Select New. PowerPoint displays the Define Custom Show dialog box.

5. Type a name for the custom slide show.

6. Select the check box beside each slide you want to include in the custom show.

7. Select Add. PowerPoint adds the selected slides to the Slides in Custom Show list.

8. Select a slide.

9. Select Up or Down to reposition the slide within the custom show.

10. Select Remove to delete the slide from the custom show.

11. Select OK to return to the Custom Shows dialog box. PowerPoint displays the name of your custom slide show in the Custom Shows list.

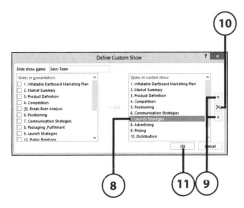

12. Select Close.

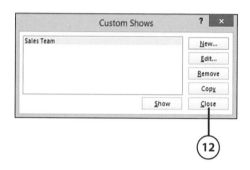

Editing a Custom Slide Show

To make changes to your custom slide show, select Slide Show, Custom Slide Show, Custom Shows, select the custom slide show, and then select Edit.

Running a Slide Show

With your slides laid out, the text perfected, and the formatting just right, you are now ready to present your slide show. The next few sections show you how to start and navigate a slide show, as well as how to set up an automatic slide show.

Starting the Slide Show

You can start a slide show from the beginning or from a particular slide.

1. If you want to start the slide show from a particular slide, select that slide.

2. Select the Slide Show tab.

3. If you rehearsed the slide show timings, as described earlier in this chapter, and you want the slides to advance automatically, select the Use Timings check box.

4. To start the slide show from the current slide, select From Current Slide; otherwise, select From Beginning. PowerPoint starts the slide show.

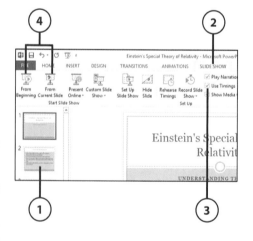

Keyboard Shortcut

You can start your slide show from the beginning by pressing F5. To start the slide show from the selected slide, instead, press Shift+F5.

>>>Go Further

STARTING A CUSTOM SLIDE SHOW

If you configured a custom slide show, as described earlier in the "Creating a Custom Slide Show" section, you can also launch that custom show. To start a custom slide show, select the Slide Show tab, select Custom Slide Show, and then select Custom Shows to open the Custom Shows dialog box. Select the show you want in the list that appears and then select Show.

Navigating Slides

With your slide show running, you now need to navigate from one slide to the next.

1. Swipe the screen from right to left. PowerPoint displays either the next slide or the next animation in the current slide.

2. Tap the screen. PowerPoint displays the slide show controls.

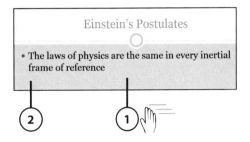

3. Tap Previous to return to the previous slide or undo the most recent animation.

4. Tap Next to move to the next slide or play the next animation.

5. Tap Pointer Options.

6. Select the type of pointer you want to use.

7. Select a pointer color.

8. Select Black Screen to turn the screen black. Select Black Screen again to return to the regular screen.

9. Select More. PowerPoint displays a menu of slide show controls.

10. Select End Show to stop the slide show before you reach the last slide.

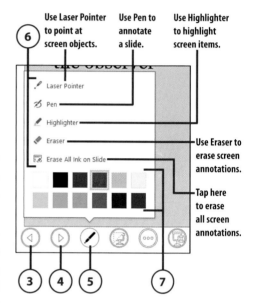

Use Laser Pointer to point at screen objects.

Use Pen to annotate a slide.

Use Highlighter to highlight screen items.

Use Eraser to erase screen annotations.

Tap here to erase all screen annotations.

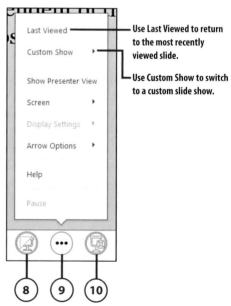

Use Last Viewed to return to the most recently viewed slide.

Use Custom Show to switch to a custom slide show.

NAVIGATING THE SLIDE SHOW FROM THE KEYBOARD

PowerPoint gives you quite a few keyboard alternatives for navigating and controlling the slide show. These are useful alternatives because displaying the shortcut menu can look unprofessional, and pressing a key or key combination is also usually faster.

Press	To
N	Advance to the next slide or animation (you can also press the spacebar, Enter, right arrow, down arrow, or Page Down keys)
P	Return to the previous slide or animation (you can also press Backspace, left arrow, up arrow, or Page Up keys)
n, Enter	Navigate to slide number *n*
S	Pause/resume an automatic slide show (you can also press plus [+])
B	Toggle black screen on and off (you can also press period [.])
W	Toggle white screen on and off (you can also press comma [,])
Ctrl+T	Display the Windows taskbar
Esc	End the slide show (you can also press hyphen [-] or Ctrl+Break)

Setting Up an Automatic Slide Show

What do you do if you want to show a presentation at a trade show, fair, or other public event, but you cannot have a person presenting the slide show? Similarly, what do you do if you want to send a presentation to a customer or prospect and you cannot be there to go through the slide show yourself? In these and similar situations, you can configure the presentation to run automatically.

1. Select the Slide Show tab.

2. Rehearse the slide show timings and save the timings when you are done.

Advancing Slides Automatically

As an alternative to rehearsing the slide show timings, for each slide in the show, select the slide, select the Transitions tab, select the After check box in the Timing group, and then use the After text box to specify the number of seconds after which you want each slide to advance.

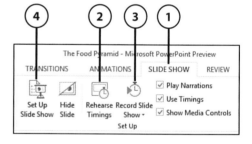

3. Add narration to the presentation.

4. Select Set Up Slide Show to display the Set Up Show dialog box.

5. Select the Browsed at a Kiosk option.

6. Select OK.

PowerPoint activates (and disables) the Using Timings, If Present option.

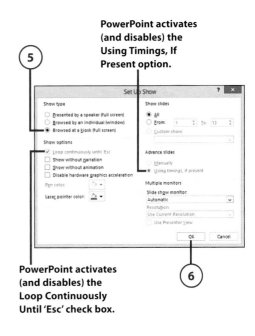

PowerPoint activates (and disables) the Loop Continuously Until 'Esc' check box.

Tag
items

Add
sections

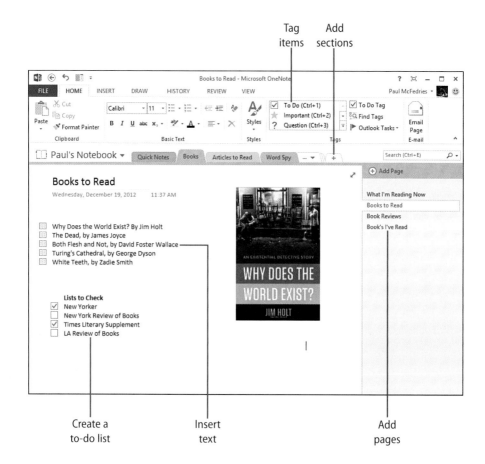

Create a
to-do list

Insert
text

Add
pages

In this chapter, you'll learn about building a OneNote notebook, working with sections and pages, entering text and lists, and tagging items.

- → Building a notebook by adding sections and pages
- → Color-coding sections and pages
- → Entering text and working with page containers
- → Tagging items on a page
- → Building a OneNote to-do list

Building a OneNote Notebook

The Office RT applications that you've learned about so far in the book—Word, Excel, and PowerPoint—enable you to enter data in a relatively structured format: Word with its sequential sentences and paragraphs; Excel with its rows, columns, and cells; and PowerPoint with its sequential slides and slide placeholders. However, the data we deal with in our lives isn't always so structured: thoughts, ideas, inspirations, to-do lists, phone numbers, names of books to read and movies to see, website and email addresses, and on and on.

Many of us keep notebooks handy for jotting down these random bits of data, but we live in an electronic age, so wouldn't it be great to be able to jot down stray bits of information in a digital format?

I'm happy to report that the answer to that question is, "You can!" The electronic version of your paper notebook is OneNote, which enables you to quickly and easily record just about anything that you'd normally scribble on a piece of paper (even doodles, as you see in Chapter 14, "Getting More Out of OneNote"). With OneNote, you can do all that and also much more:

- Paste pictures, clip art, and text

- Insert links to websites

- Organize data into tables

- Share your notes with other people

In this chapter, you'll learn how to use the OneNote to build a notebook and add some basic items such as text and bulleted lists. See Chapter 14 to learn how to augment your notebooks with links, files, digital ink, and more.

Working with Sections

In the real world, a notebook might come with (or you might add) several tabs that divide the notebook into separate sections, each with its own collection of pages. This is the metaphor that OneNote uses. OneNote files are called *notebooks*, and each notebook consists of a series of *sections*, and each section consists of one or more *pages*. You use these pages to enter your free-form notes and other data, such as links and images.

A notebook is a collection of different types of data scraps from a variety of sources. It's important to impose some kind of order on all those scraps so that the notebook doesn't devolve into an unruly mess where it takes too long to find what you need.

Within each notebook, the main level of organization is the section, which is represented by a tab in the left pane of the notebook. You use the sections to break down the notebook's overall topic or theme into smaller subjects. You can create as many sections as you need because there's no practical limit on the number of sections you can add to a notebook.

OneNote 2013 is a hierarchical storage system, with notebooks at the top level, sections at the second level, and pages at the third level. You can fine-tune this hierarchy by taking advantage of OneNote's color-coding features, which enable you to link similar items visually by applying the same color to those items.

Inserting a New Section

When you create a new notebook using OneNote, the resulting file has a single section that contains a single page. However, you are free to add more sections as needed.

1. Open the notebook you want to work with.

2. Select the Create a New Section icon. OneNote creates the new section and displays the section name in a text box.

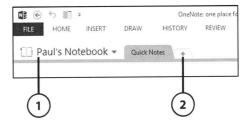

Keyboard Shortcut

You can also create a new section by pressing Ctrl+T.

---

3. Type the section name.

4. Tap an empty part of the new section. OneNote closes the text box.

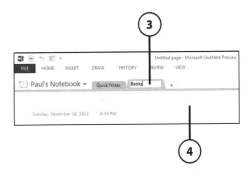

Renaming a Section

If you made an error when you originally named a section, or if the section's current name no longer reflects the section's content, you can rename the section.

1. Tap and hold the section tab for several seconds, then release. OneNote displays a shortcut menu of section-related commands.

2. Tap Rename.

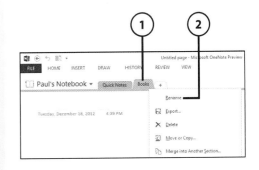

3. Type the section name.

4. Tap an empty part of the new section. OneNote closes the text box.

Moving a Section

OneNote adds each new section to the right of the existing section tabs. To move a section, tap and drag the section's tab left or right until the section is in the position you want and then release the tab.

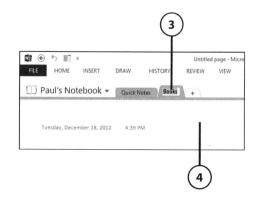

Color-Coding a Section

Color-coding a section means that you apply a specified color that appears in the section's tab (as well as the area surrounding the section when you select the section). So if a notebook contains two or more sections that are similar, you can informally relate them to one another by applying the same color.

1. For a few seconds, tap and hold the tab of the section you want to color. OneNote displays a shortcut menu of section-related commands.

2. Select Section Color.

3. Select the color you want to apply. OneNote applies the color to the section.

Using Similar Colors Across Notebooks

If you use multiple notebooks, it's a good idea to apply the same color to the same kinds of pages in each notebook. For example, if all your notebooks have a To-Do List section, it makes navigating the notebooks easier if those sections all use the same color.

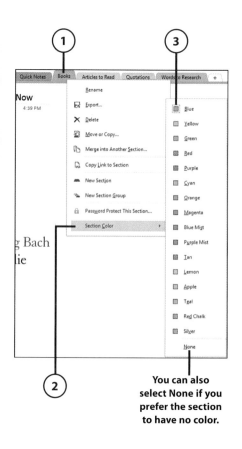

You can also select None if you prefer the section to have no color.

Working with Pages

After sections, the second level in the notebook organizational hierarchy is the *page*, which is more or less a blank slate into which you insert your OneNote data. Each section can have an unlimited number of pages, and the idea is that you use separate pages to break down each section into separate subtopics. Each page appears in the right pane of the notebook window.

Inserting a New Page

Each new section you create comes with a new page, but you can add more pages whenever you need them.

1. Select the section in which you want to insert the new page.

2. Select Add Page. OneNote inserts a new page into the section.

Keyboard Shortcut

You can also add a new page to the current section by pressing Ctrl+N.

---

3. Type the page title.

Moving a Page

OneNote adds each new page to the bottom of the existing page tabs. To move a page, tap and drag the page's tab up or down until the page is in the position you want, then release the tab.

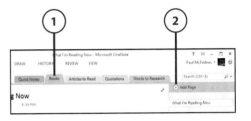

To insert a new page below an existing page, tap and hold the existing page and then select New Page.

The page title appears in the page tab.

Inserting a New Page from a Template

OneNote offers a collection of page templates that enable you to insert a page that comes with preset text and formatting for things like lecture notes, business meetings, and to-do lists.

1. Select the section in which you want to insert the new page.

2. Select the Insert tab.

3. Select Page Templates.

4. Select Page Templates. OneNote displays the Templates task pane.

5. Select a category.

6. Select the page template you want to use.

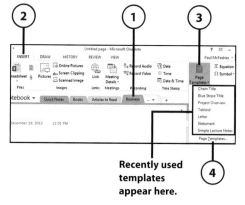

Recently used templates appear here.

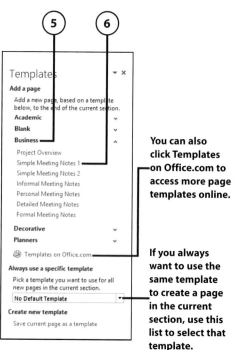

You can also click Templates on Office.com to access more page templates online.

If you always want to use the same template to create a page in the current section, use this list to select that template.

>>>Go Further

SAVING A PAGE AS A TEMPLATE

If you find yourself using similar text and formatting for many of your pages, you can save yourself quite a bit of work by saving that text and formatting as a page template that you can apply using the steps in this section. To save the current page as a template, select Insert, Page Templates, Page Templates to open the Templates task pane. At the bottom of the pane, select Save Current Page as a Template to open the Save As Template dialog box. Type a name for the template. If you always want to use this template to create a page in the current section, select the Set as Default Template… check box. Select Save.

Entering Text on a Page

Filling your pages with content is what OneNote is all about, and OneNote makes it easy to insert everything from simple typewritten or handwritten notes, dates and times, image files, screen captures, and even entire files. All OneNote content appears inside a *container*, which is essentially a box that surrounds the content. After you have some content inside a container, you can move the container around on the page, edit or format the container content, split the content into multiple containers, and more.

Most page content consists of text notes, and OneNote makes it very simple to add text to a page:

- For typewritten notes, tap where you want the note to appear and then start typing. OneNote immediately places a container around the text. When you're done, select outside the container.

- To create a bulleted list, tap where you want the list to appear and then select Home, Bullets. You can also select Home, Numbering if you prefer a numbered list.

- To add text from a document, open the document, copy the text, return to OneNote, tap inside the page where you want the text to appear, and then paste the copied text.

See Chapter 14 to learn how to add more types of content to a page.

Working with Page Containers

When you insert data on a page—whether it's text, a link, an image, or clip art—the data appears inside a special object called a *container*. When you have one or more containers on a page, working with the data is almost always straightforward. For example, to edit container text, you select inside the container and change the existing text or add new text. To format the text, you select it and use the buttons in the Ribbon's Home tab.

Selecting Container Text

To quickly select all the text in a container, double-tap the top edge of the container.

You'll probably spend a significant amount of time in OneNote adjusting containers from one part of a page to another to get the best or most efficient layout for your data. Here are the basic techniques to use:

- **Moving a container**—Select the container to display its frame. Drag the top edge of the container and drop it on the new position.

- **Sizing a container**—Select the container to display the selection handles on the corners and sides. Drag a selection handle to get the width you want.

Building a OneNote Table

A typical notebook page, like a typical page in a paper notebook, is a jumble of text, with placeholders scattered around the page. This randomness isn't necessarily a bad thing because it's in keeping with OneNote's inherent informality and (at least on the surface) structure-free format. However, there will be times when you *want* your notes to have some structure. If it's a list of items, you can insert a bulleted list into a placeholder (on the Home tab, click Bullets); if it's an ordered sequence of items, use a numbered list, instead (on the Home tab, click Numbering).

However, you might have data that consists of multiple items, each of which has the same set of details. For example, you might want to record a list of upcoming flights, each of which has an airline name, flight number, departure date and time, destination, arrival date and time, seat number, and so on.

For these kinds of data structures, you can insert a table into a container. A table is a rectangular structure with the following characteristics:

- Each item in the list gets its own horizontal rectangle called a *row*.

- Each set of details in the list gets its own vertical rectangle called a *column*.

- The rectangle formed by the intersection of a row and a column is called a *cell* and you use the table cells to hold the data.

In other words, a OneNote table is very similar to an Excel worksheet (and a Word table, which I discussed in Chapter 5, "Working with Page Layout in Word").

Inserting a Table

When you want to construct a table in OneNote, your first step is to create the empty table structure that specifies the number of rows and columns you want in your table. So you need to examine your data and figure out how many items there are (that value will be the number of rows you need in your table), and how many details you want to record for each item (that value will be the number of columns you need in your table). Once you've done that, you're ready to insert the table.

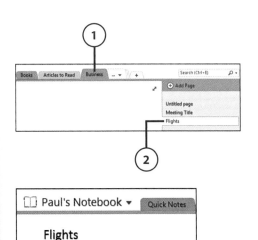

1. Select the section that contains the page you want to work with.

2. Select the page in which you want to insert the table.

3. Select where you want the table to appear.

4. Select the Insert tab.

5. Select Table. OneNote displays the Insert Table gallery.

6. Select Insert Table to display the Insert Table dialog box.

7. Specify the number of columns you want in your table.

8. Specify the number of rows you want in the table.

9. Select OK. OneNote inserts the table.

For a small table, you can also tap a box that represents the number of rows and columns you want.

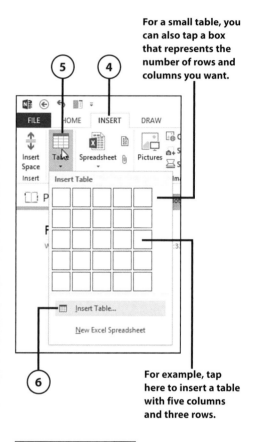

For example, tap here to insert a table with five columns and three rows.

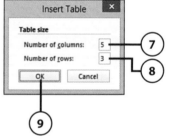

10. Type your text into the table cells.

Use the tools on the Layout tab to work with your table.

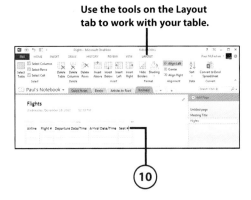

(10)

Working with a OneNote Table

A OneNote table is very similar to a Word table, so you can use the same techniques to add and delete rows and columns, select table items, and so on. See Chapter 5 for the details.

Working with Tags

OneNote enables you to augment items in a page with small icons called *tags*. For example, many tags can help you prioritize page data, including the Important, Critical, and Question tags. Similarly, many tags can help you organize your data, including the Project A and Project B tags.

However, probably the most common use of tags is to set up a to-do list. One of the secrets of productivity in a fast-paced, information-overloaded world is organizing the things that require your attention and your effort in a way that minimizes stress and maximizes efficiency. If you have a long list of things to do, the worst way to handle the list is to keep it in your head. If you do this, you'll not only worry about forgetting something, but you'll always have each task rumbling around in your brain, so you'll jump from one to the other rather than concentrating on a single task at a time. Plastering sticky notes all over your monitor isn't much better because all the tasks are still "in your face," and you won't be much better off.

The best way to organize a list of pending and current tasks is to have a single place where you record the tasks' particulars and can augment those particulars as things change and new data becomes available. This place must be one that you check regularly so that there's never a danger of overlooking a task, and ideally it should be a place where you can prioritize your tasks. This way, you can focus on a single task, knowing that everything you need to do is safely recorded and prioritized. As you've probably guessed by now, the place I'm talking about is OneNote, which is ideally suited to recording, organizing, and prioritizing tasks and to-do lists.

Tagging an Item

You can apply a tag to a single item, multiple items, or to every item within a container. You can also apply multiple tags to a single item.

1. Select the section that contains the page you want to work with.

2. Select the page that contains the data you want to tag.

3. If you want to tag a specific paragraph within a text container, select inside that paragraph. If you want to apply the same tag to multiple paragraphs, select those paragraphs. If you want to apply the same tag to every paragraph, tap the top edge of the container to select all the text.

4. Select the Home tab.

5. Select More in the Tags group. OneNote displays the Tags gallery.

6. Select the tag you want to use. OneNote applies the tag to the data.

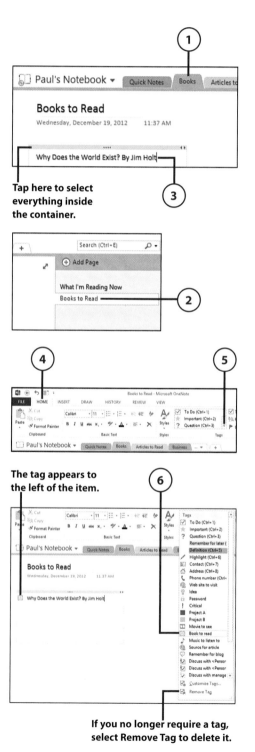

Tap here to select everything inside the container.

The tag appears to the left of the item.

If you no longer require a tag, select Remove Tag to delete it.

>>>Go Further

CREATING A CUSTOM TAG

If none of the default OneNote tags is just right for your needs, you can create a custom tag. Open the Tags gallery and select the Customize Tags command. In the Customize Tags dialog box, select New Tag to open the New Tag dialog box. Type a name for your custom tag. Use the Symbol, Font Color, and Highlight Color lists to construct your custom tag, and then click OK.

Building Lists

To-do lists are an important part of OneNote, and part of the evidence for that is the large number of check box–like tags it offers. Besides the standard To Do tag, there are eight others:

- Discuss with <Person A>
- Discuss with <Person B>
- Discuss with Manager
- Schedule Meeting
- Call Back
- To Do Priority 1
- To Do Priority 2
- Client Request

Each of these tags gives you a check box augmented with a small icon. When you complete a task, you select the check box to place a red check mark inside, which gives you a strong visual clue about which tasks are done and which are still pending.

Creating a To-Do List

You create a OneNote to-do list by
building a list and then tagging it
using the To Do tag.

1. Select the section that contains
   the page you want to work with.

2. Select the page where you want
   your to-do list to appear.

3. Type each item in your to-do list.

4. Tap the top edge of the container
   to select the entire to-do list.

5. Select the Home tab.

6. Select More in the Tags group.
   OneNote displays the Tags gallery.

7. Select the To Do tag. OneNote
   applies the tag to the data.

Keyboard Shortcut

You can also apply the To Do tag
by pressing Ctrl+1.

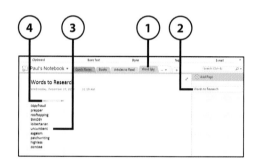

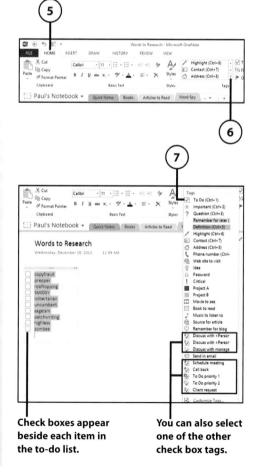

Check boxes appear
beside each item in
the to-do list.

You can also select
one of the other
check box tags.

Insert file
attachments

Insert
spreadsheets

Insert links
to OneNote
locations

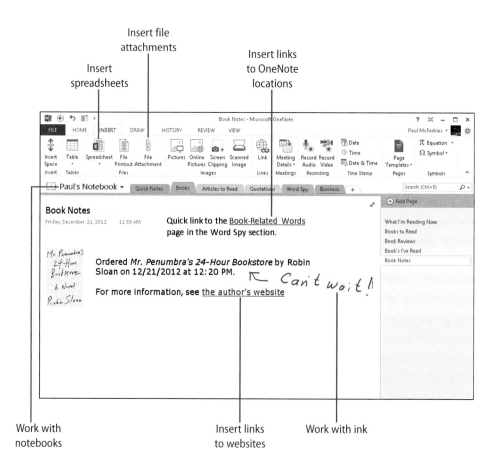

Work with
notebooks

Insert links
to websites

Work with ink

In this chapter, you'll learn how to get more out of OneNote notebooks, including creating new notebooks, inserting links and files, and adding ink to a page.

→ Creating new notebooks

→ Inserting the date and time

→ Adding links to a page

→ Inserting spreadsheets and other files

→ Annotating a page with written text and other ink

Getting More Out of OneNote

You learned the basics of working with OneNote in Chapter 13, "Building a OneNote Notebook," but there's much more the program can do. In this chapter, you'll extend your OneNote education by learning a few more useful tasks, such as creating new notebooks, adding data such as the current date and time and links to other objects, and inserting files on a page. Because you're running OneNote on a Windows 8 tablet, you'll also populate and annotate a page by writing directly on the screen, and you'll learn how to use this "ink" later in this chapter.

Working with Notebooks

The hierarchical structure of a OneNote notebook means that you can break down your data in a number of ways. That is, you can assign major topics their own sections, and then subdivide each topic into multiple pages within a section. That works well for most people, and it's common to use only a single notebook. However, you might find that your notebook has so many sections that it has become difficult to navigate and to find the data you need. In that case, you might consider creating a second notebook. For example, many people maintain one notebook for personal data and another for business data. Similarly, if you share your computer with other people but haven't set up separate user accounts, then you'll no doubt prefer that everyone use their own notebook.

Creating a New Notebook

You can create a new notebook either locally on your PC, or remotely on your SkyDrive. For the latter, you need to be logged in to Windows 8 using your Microsoft account.

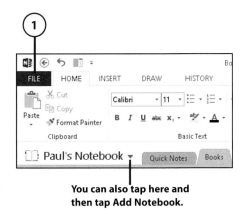

1. Select the File tab.

2. Select New.

3. Select your SkyDrive.

4. Type a name for the notebook.

5. Select Create Notebook. OneNote creates the new notebook and then asks if you want to share it.

6. Select I Am Done for Now.

You can also tap here and then tap Add Notebook.

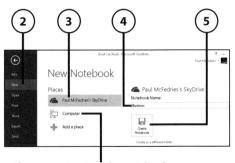

If you want to store the notebook locally, select Computer, instead.

Sharing

To learn how to share data through SkyDrive, see "Collaborating with SkyDrive" in Chapter 16, "Collaborating with Others."

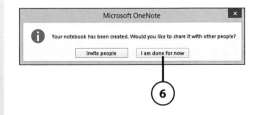

Switching Between Notebooks

Once you have two or more notebooks open, OneNote gives you a quick and easy method for switching from one to another.

1. Select the name of the current notebook. OneNote displays the Notebook pane.

2. Select the notebook you want to use. OneNote switches to that workbook.

Closing a Workbook

If you no longer want a particular notebook to appear in the Notebook pane, you need to close it. Display the Notebook pane, tap and hold for a few seconds on the notebook you want to close, and then select Close This Notebook.

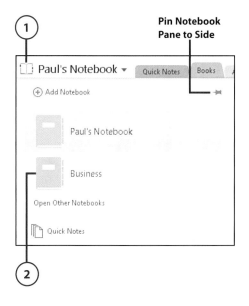

Pin Notebook Pane to Side

PINNING THE NOTEBOOK PANE

If you find that you often switch from one notebook to another, you can make the switching process even easier by opening the Notebook pane and then tapping Pin Notebook Pane to Side (the pin icon that appears in the upper-right corner of the pane). This tells OneNote to always display the Notebook pane on the left side of the window, so you can switch to any open notebook just by tapping it.

If you later decide that the Notebook pane is taking up too much room, you can hide it again by tapping Unpin Notebook Pane from Side (the vertical pin icon that appears in the upper-right corner of the Notebook pane).

>>>Go Further

Setting Notebook Properties

A notebook's properties control the name of the notebook and the color the notebook appears in the Notebook pane. You can access the notebook's properties to change one or both of these settings.

1. Select the File tab.

2. Select Info.

3. Select Settings for the notebook you want to modify.

4. Select Properties. The Notebook Properties dialog box opens.

5. Use the Display Name text box to change the notebook's name.

6. Select the Color drop-down list and then select a notebook color.

7. Select OK. OneNote applies the new property values.

Accessing the Notebook Properties

Another way to access a notebook's properties is to display the Notebook pane, tap and hold the notebook for a few seconds, and then select Properties.

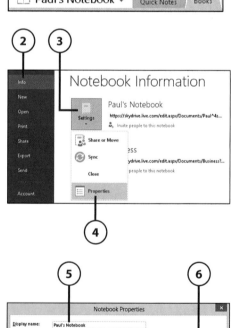

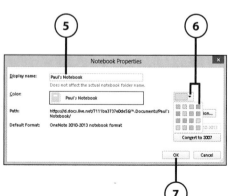

Adding Data to a Page

The straightforward tap-and-type nature of a OneNote page makes it easy to add simple notes, lists, and other text snippets. And, of course, you're free to take advantage of the techniques you learned in Chapter 3, "Working with Office RT Graphics," to populate a page with pictures, clip art, SmartArt, WordArt, and shapes. The inherent free-form approach offered by OneNote also means that there are plenty of other data types you can add to a page. The most common of these are the date and time, links, Excel worksheets, and files, each of which is described in the next few sections.

Inserting the Date and Time

Some of the content you add to a OneNote page will be date- and/or time-sensitive. For such content, you should date- and/or time-stamp the placeholder by inserting the current date, time, or both.

1. Select the section you want to use.

2. Select the page you want to use.

3. Position the insertion point where you want to insert the date.

4. Select the Insert tab.

5. Select Date. OneNote inserts today's date.

Keyboard Shortcut

You can also insert today's date by pressing Alt+Shift+D.

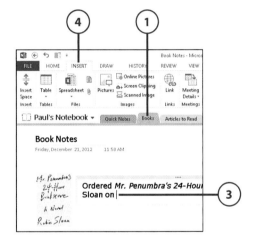

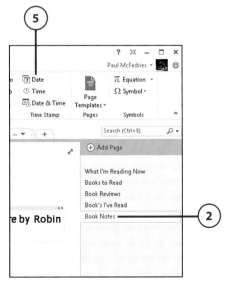

6. Position the insertion point where you want to insert the time.

7. Select Time. OneNote inserts the current time.

Keyboard Shortcut

You can also insert the current time by pressing Alt+Shift+T.

To insert both the date and time at once, select Date & Time.

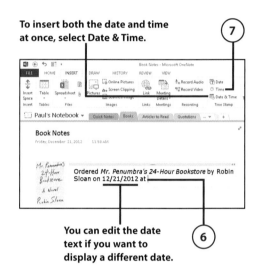

You can edit the date text if you want to display a different date.

Adding a Link to a Website

OneNote comes with a Links command that enables you to insert links to websites. This is very handy if you use your pages to store links to websites you visit often or want to visit in the future. (For the latter, apply the Web Site to Visit tag; see Chapter 13.)

1. Select the section you want to use.

2. Select the page you want to use.

3. Position the insertion point where you want to insert the link. You can also select existing text that you want to turn into a link.

4. Select the Insert tab.

5. Select Link. OneNote displays the Link dialog box.

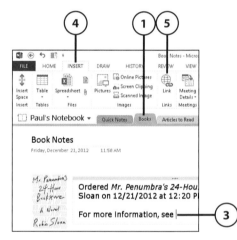

Keyboard Shortcut

You can also display the Link dialog box by pressing Ctrl+K.

6. If you didn't select text in advance, type the link text.

7. Type the link address.

8. Select OK. OneNote inserts the link.

Editing a Link

To make changes to a link, tap and hold the link for a few seconds to display the Mini Toolbar, tap the drop-down arrow, and then tap Edit Link.

Adding a Link to a OneNote Location

Besides linking to a website, OneNote also enables you to create a link to another OneNote location: a notebook, a section within a notebook, a page within a section, or even a note within a page. This makes navigating OneNote extremely easy because you can select a link to jump instantly to that location.

1. Select the section you want to use.

2. Select the page you want to use.

3. Select the text that you want to turn into a link. You can also position the insertion point where you want to insert the link.

4. Select the Insert tab.

5. Select Link. OneNote displays the Link dialog box.

You can also click Browse the Web to select the web page using a browser.

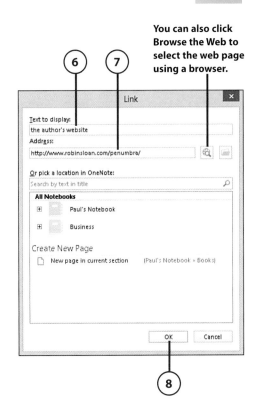

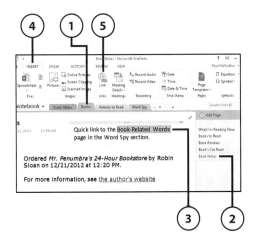

Quick link to the Book-Related Words page in the Word Spy section.

Keyboard Shortcut

You can also display the Link dialog box by pressing Ctrl+K.

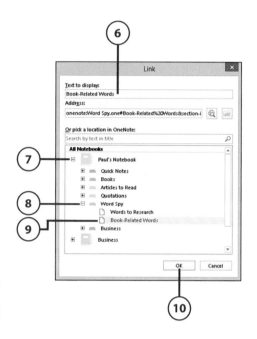

6. If you didn't select text in advance, type the link text.

7. Select the notebook you want to use.

8. If you want to link to a section, select the section.

9. If you want to link to a page, select the page.

10. Select OK. OneNote inserts the link.

EASIER LOCATION LINKS

If you find yourself inserting lots of location links in your notebooks, OneNote offers several methods that make it even easier to create such links:

- To link to a notebook, tap and hold the notebook title for a few seconds and then click Copy Link to Notebook.

- To link to a section, tap and hold the section tab for a few seconds and then click Copy Link to Section.

- To link to a page, tap and hold the page tab for a few seconds and then click Copy Link to Page.

- To link to a note, tap and hold the note container for a few seconds and then click Copy Link to Paragraph.

Then position the insertion point where you want the link to appear, select the Home tab, and then select Paste.

Inserting a Spreadsheet File

If you have an existing Excel workbook that you'd like to view within OneNote, you can insert the file on a page.

1. Select the section you want to use.

2. Select the page you want to use.

3. Position the insertion point where you want the spreadsheet file to appear.

4. Select the Insert tab.

5. Select Spreadsheet.

6. Select Existing Excel Spreadsheet. OneNote displays the Choose Document to Insert dialog box.

7. Select a location.

8. Select the spreadsheet file you want to insert.

9. Select Insert. OneNote displays the Insert File dialog box.

10. Select Insert Spreadsheet. OneNote inserts the workbook data into the page.

11. To work with the spreadsheet, select Edit to open the file in Excel.

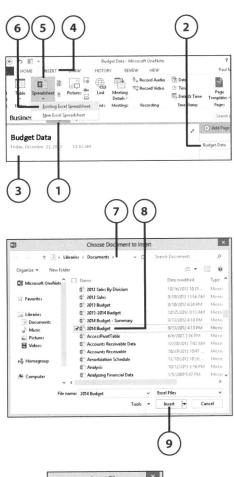

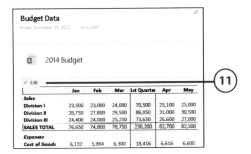

Inserting a New Spreadsheet

If you don't have an existing spreadsheet you want to insert, you can instead insert a new spreadsheet.

1. Select the section you want to use.

2. Select the page you want to use.

3. Position the insertion point where you want the spreadsheet file to appear.

4. Select the Insert tab.

5. Select Spreadsheet.

6. Select New Excel Spreadsheet. OneNote inserts the new spreadsheet.

7. To work with the spreadsheet, select Edit to open the file in Excel.

Attaching a File

If you want quick access to any type of file, you can attach that file to a OneNote page.

1. Select the section you want to use.

2. Select the page you want to use.

3. Select where you want the file icon to appear.

4. Select the Insert tab.

5. Select File Attachment. OneNote displays the Choose a File or a Set of Files to Insert dialog box.

If you want to display a file's contents instead of an icon, select File Printout.

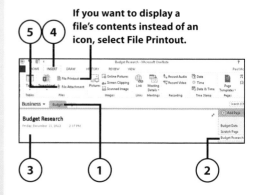

6. Select a location.

7. Select the spreadsheet file you want to insert.

8. Select Insert. OneNote inserts an icon for the file into the page.

9. To work with the file, double-tap it. OneNote displays a warning dialog box.

10. Select OK. The file opens in its default application.

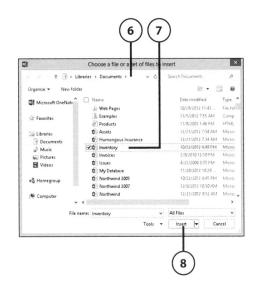

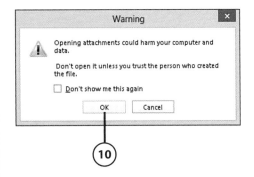

Adding Ink

Office RT implements *ink integration*, which means that an object type called *digital ink* or, simply, *ink* is part of the Office system, like the AutoShape and Text Box object types, for instance. In fact, ink objects are part of the Office drawing layer that holds AutoShapes, text boxes, WordArt, pictures, and so on, and you can format ink like other drawing layer objects by changing, for example, the text color and line weight.

Ink enables you to mark up OneNote pages using your finger or a digital pen or stylus. This enables you to annotate a page directly, which means either writing notes using your own handwriting or adding highlighting, diagrams, proofreader marks, or other symbols. You can even convert ink text into regular text.

Handwriting Text

For quick notes, you can use your finger or a digital pen to handwrite notes directly on a page.

1. Tap the section you want to use.

2. Tap the page you want to use.

3. Tap the Draw tab.

4. Tap the More button in the Tools group. OneNote displays the Tools gallery.

5. Tap the pen you want to use.

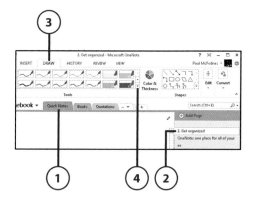

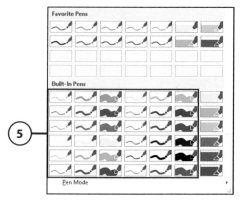

6. Use your finger or digital pen to handwrite directly on the screen.

You can tap Color & Thickness to gain more control of the color and size of the ink.

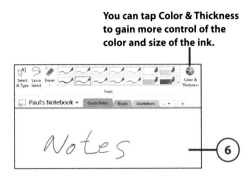

Highlighting Text

To emphasize text on a page, you can use your finger or digital pen to apply a highlight to the text.

1. Tap the section you want to use.

2. Tap the page you want to use.

3. Tap the Draw tab.

4. Tap the More button in the Tools group. OneNote displays the Tools gallery.

5. Tap the highlighter you want to use.

6. Use your finger or digital pen to tap and drag across the text you want highlighted.

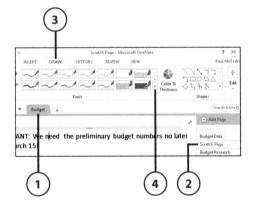

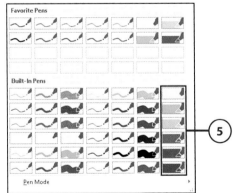

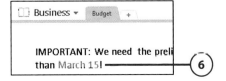

Converting Ink to Text

Handwriting text is quick and easy, but it suffers from some major drawbacks: It can't be searched, spell-checked, or used in any program that doesn't support ink. To work around these problems, you need to convert your handwriting to digital text.

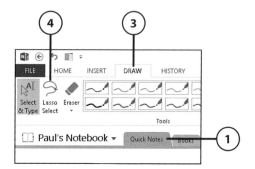

1. Tap the section you want to use.

2. Tap the page you want to use.

3. Tap the Draw tab.

4. Tap Lasso Select.

5. Position your finger or the digital stylus above and to the left of the ink you want to convert.

6. Draw a clockwise circle around the ink.

7. When the text is completely within the lasso, release the screen. OneNote selects the ink.

8. Tap Ink to Text. OneNote converts the selected handwriting to digital text.

Faster Ink Conversions

In many cases, an even easier way to convert ink to text is to tap and hold the ink for a few seconds to display the Mini Toolbar, tap the drop-down arrow, tap Convert Ink, and then tap Ink to Text.

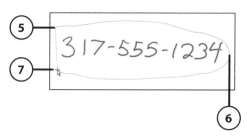

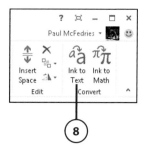

Erasing Ink

If you have ink you no longer need,
or if you've made some stray marks
on the page, you can erase the ink.

1. Tap the section you want to use.

2. Tap the page you want to use.

3. Tap the Draw tab.

4. Tap Eraser.

5. Tap Stroke Eraser.

6. Tap the ink stroke you want to
   erase. OneNote removes the
   stroke. Repeat as necessary.

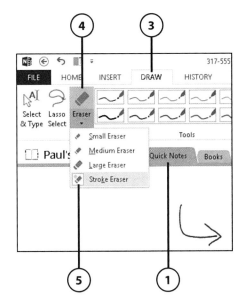

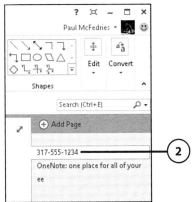

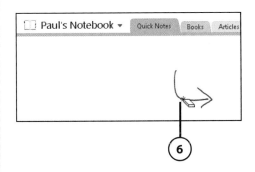

Customize the Quick
Access Toolbar

Add Ribbon commands to
the Quick Access Toolbar

Change the
background

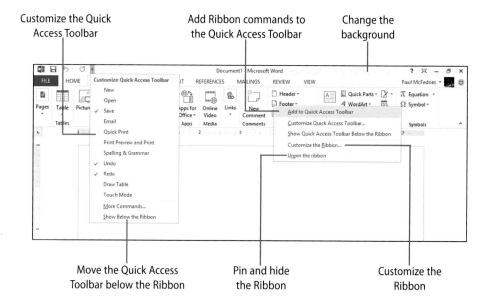

Move the Quick Access
Toolbar below the Ribbon

Pin and hide
the Ribbon

Customize the
Ribbon

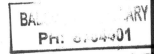

In this chapter, you'll learn about customizing the Office RT applications, including working with the application options and customizing the interface.

→ Accessing the Options dialog box for the Office RT applications
→ Changing your Office RT user name and initials
→ Pinning, hiding, and customizing the Ribbon
→ Positioning and customizing the Quick Access Toolbar
→ Changing the background for the Office RT applications

Customizing the Office RT Applications

This book is called *My Office RT*, so it's time you learned how to put the "My" in Office RT. I speak, of course, about customizing the applications in some way. After all, the interface and settings that you see when you first use Office RT are the "factory defaults." That is, how the program looks and how it works out of the box have been specified by Microsoft. However, this "official" version of the program is almost always designed with some mythical "average" user in mind. Nothing is wrong with this concept, but it almost certainly means that the program is not set up optimally for *you*. This chapter shows you how to get the most out of the Office RT programs—Word, Excel, PowerPoint, and OneNote—by performing a few customization chores to set up the program to suit the way you work.

Working with Application Options

Customizing Word, Excel, PowerPoint, and OneNote most often means tweaking a setting or two in the Options dialog box that comes with each program. Each program has a unique Options dialog box configuration, so it's beyond the scope of this book to discuss these dialog boxes in detail. Instead, I'll introduce you to them by showing you how to get them onscreen and by going through some useful settings.

Working with the Options Dialog Box

You'll often find some need to access the Options dialog box for an Office RT application, so let's begin by quickly reviewing the steps required to access and work with this dialog box in your current Office RT program.

1. Select File. The Office RT application, Excel in this example, displays the File menu.

2. Select Options. The Office RT application opens the Options dialog box.

3. Select a tab. The Office RT application displays the options related to the selected tab.

4. Use the controls to tweak the application's settings.

5. Select OK. The Office RT application puts the changed options into effect.

Keyboard Shortcut

You can also open the Options dialog box in any Office RT application by pressing Alt+F, T.

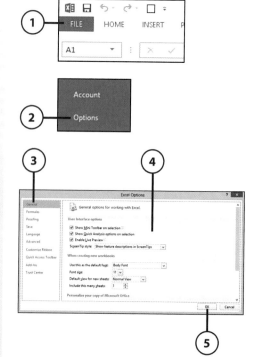

Changing Your User Name and Initials

In Chapter 16, "Collaborating with Others," you'll learn how to insert comments into a document and to track document changes. In both cases, the underlying program keeps a record of each "reviewer" who made changes to the document. For revisions, the program identifies the reviewer by his or her Office RT user name; for comments, the program identifies the reviewer by his or her Office RT initials. You can change both your user name and your initials to whatever you prefer.

1. Select File to open the File menu.

2. Select Options to open the Options dialog box.

3. Select the General tab.

4. Use the User Name text box to type your user name.

5. In Word, PowerPoint, and OneNote, use the Initials text box to type your initials.

6. Select OK. Office RT puts the new user name and initials into effect.

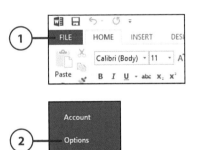

Universal User Name and Initials

Your user name and initials are universal in Office RT. That is, changing your user name or initials in one program automatically means the new user name or initials will appear in the other Office RT programs.

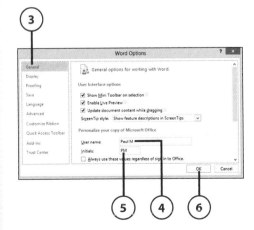

APPLYING YOUR USER NAME AND INITIALS ACROSS ACCOUNTS

If you have multiple Microsoft accounts, you might still want to use the same user name and initials no matter which account you're currently signed in with. You can configure Office RT to do this by opening the Options dialog box in any Office RT application, selecting the General tab, and then selecting the Always Use These Values Regardless of Sign In to Office check box. Select OK to put the setting into effect.

Bypassing the Start Screen at Launch

By default, Word, Excel, and PowerPoint display the Start screen when you first launch the application, which lets you choose a template for a new file or select a recently used file. If you almost always opt to open a blank document, workbook, or presentation at startup, you can make this the default behavior.

1. Launch the Office RT application you want to customize.

2. Select File to open the File menu.

3. Select Options to open the Options dialog box.

4. Select the General tab.

5. Deselect the Show the Start Screen When This Application Starts check box.

6. Select OK. The Office RT application puts the setting into effect.

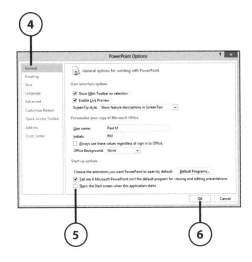

Customizing the Interface

Besides the work area of any Office RT application window, the Office RT interface mostly consists of the Ribbon and its associated Quick Access Toolbar. These two elements are the royal road to all things Office RT, so you'll be less efficient and less productive if these elements aren't set up to suit the way you work.

Pinning the Ribbon

By default, the Office RT applications hide the Ribbon to give you maximum screen real estate for your documents, and you display the Ribbon by tapping any tab. If you find that extra tap to be a pain, you can avoid it by pinning the Ribbon so that it appears on screen full-time.

1. Tap any Ribbon tab to display the Ribbon.

2. Tap Pin the Ribbon. The Ribbon appears onscreen full-time.

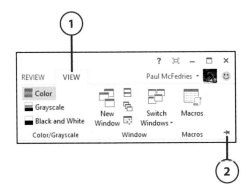

Shortcuts for Pinning the Ribbon

The Office RT applications give you two shortcut methods for pinning the Ribbon: Either double-tap any Ribbon tab or press Ctrl+F1. Note that to access the function keys using the onscreen keyboard, you must use the standard keyboard layout. (In the Charms menu, tap Settings, tap Change PC Settings, tap General, and then tap the Make the Standard keyboard Layout Available switch to On.)

Hiding the Ribbon

If you followed the steps in the previous section to display the Ribbon all the time, you might later decide that you refer to the extra screen space over the convenience and opt to revert back to hiding the Ribbon until needed.

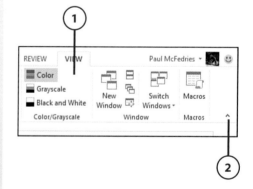

1. Tap any Ribbon tab to display the Ribbon.

2. Tap Unpin the Ribbon. The Office RT application hides the Ribbon.

Shortcuts for Unpinning the Ribbon

As with pinning, Office RT gives you two shortcuts for unpinning the Ribbon: Either double-tap any Ribbon tab or press Ctrl+F1.

Customizing the Ribbon

The Ribbon is a handy tool because it enables you to run Office commands with just a few taps of the screen. However, the Ribbon doesn't include every command for a given Office RT app. If there's a command that you use frequently, you should add it to the Ribbon for easy access.

1. In the Office RT application you want to customize, select File.

2. Select Options. The Options dialog box opens.

3. Select the Customize Ribbon tab.

Faster Access to the Customize Ribbon Tab

A quicker route to the Customize Ribbon tab is to tap and hold any part of the Ribbon and then select Customize the Ribbon.

---

4. Select the tab you want to customize.

5. Select New Group. The Office RT application adds the group.

6. Select Rename.

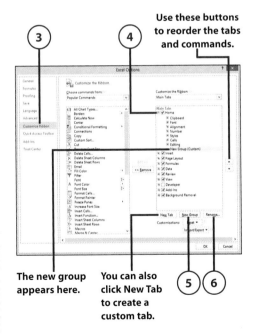

Use these buttons to reorder the tabs and commands.

The new group appears here.

You can also click New Tab to create a custom tab.

7. Type a name for the group.

8. Select OK.

9. Use the Choose Commands From list to select the command category you want to use.

10. Select the command you want to add.

11. Select the custom group or tab to which you want to add the command.

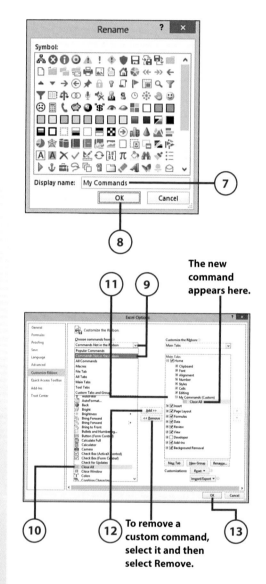

The new command appears here.

To remove a custom command, select it and then select Remove.

Customizing Tool Tabs

The tabs that appear only when you select an object are called *tool tabs*, and you can add custom groups and commands to any tool tab. Drop down the Customize the Ribbon list, select Tool Tabs, and then select the tool tab you want to customize.

12. Select Add. The Office RT application adds the command to the custom group or tab. Repeat steps 9 to 12 as needed.

13. Select OK. The Office RT application adds the new groups and commands to the Ribbon.

EXPORTING RIBBON CUSTOMIZATIONS

Customizing the Ribbon or the Quick Access Toolbar is not a difficult process, but it can be time consuming, particularly if you want to make a substantial number of changes. If you use the same Office RT application on another computer, it's likely that you'll want to have the same customizations on the other computer so that you are dealing with a consistent interface no matter where you do your work. Rather than wasting valuable time repeating the same customization steps on the other computer, you can export your customizations to a file. You can then import that file on the other computer, and the Office RT application will automatically apply the customizations for you.

In the Customize Ribbon tab of the Options dialog box, select Import/ Export and then select Export All Customizations. In the File Save dialog box, select a location for the customization file, type a name for the file, and then select Save. Select OK to close the Options dialog box.

To apply the Ribbon customizations on another computer running the same Office RT application, you need to import the customization file. Note, however, that importing a customization file replaces any existing customizations that you have created. Display the Customize Ribbon tab of the Options dialog box, select Import/Export and then select Import Customization File. In the File Open dialog box, locate and then select the customization file, and then select Open. When the application asks you to confirm that all of your existing customizations will be replaced, select Yes and then select OK.

Changing the Position of the Quick Access Toolbar

The Quick Access Toolbar offers one-tap access to common commands such as Save and Undo. By default, the Quick Access Toolbar appears above the Ribbon. This spot is good if you only have a few commands on the Quick Access Toolbar because the relatively small size of the Quick Access Toolbar means that the host Office RT program has enough room to display the document title and application name. If you want to load up the Quick Access Toolbar with lots of commands, then you should consider moving it below the Ribbon. Doing so gives the Quick Access Toolbar the full width of the window, although it does reduce the amount of space available for your document content.

1. Select Customize Quick Access Toolbar.

2. Select Show Below the Ribbon. The Office RT application moves the Quick Access Toolbar below the Ribbon.

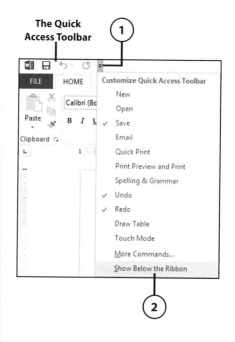

The Quick Access Toolbar

Customizing the Quick Access Toolbar

To get the most out of the Quick Access Toolbar, you need to populate it with the commands that you use most often. Note that you are not restricted to just a few commands. If you place the Quick Access Toolbar below the Ribbon, as described in the previous section, then you can use the full width of the window, plus you get a More Controls button at the end of the toolbar that enables you to display a whole other row of commands.

1. If the command you want to add is on the Ribbon, tap and hold the command and then select Add to Quick Access Toolbar.

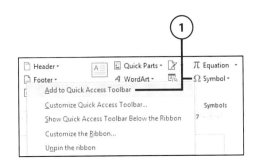

Adding a Gallery to the Toolbar

You can add a Ribbon gallery to the Quick Access Toolbar. Use the Ribbon to open the gallery, tap and hold any item in the gallery, and then select Add Gallery to Quick Access Toolbar.

Adding a Group to the Toolbar

Conveniently, you can also add entire groups to the toolbar. To add a group, tap and hold the group name in the Ribbon and then click Add to Quick Access Toolbar.

2. Select Customize Quick Access Toolbar.

3. Select More Commands. The Office RT application opens the Options dialog box with the Quick Access Toolbar tab displayed.

If the command you want to add appears in this list, select it to add it to the Quick Access Toolbar.

Commands already on the Quick Access Toolbar appear with check marks.

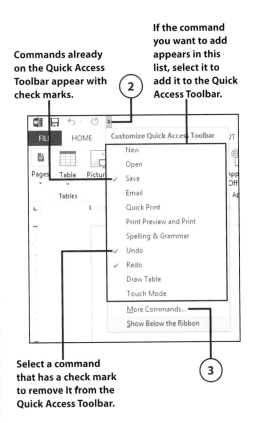

Select a command that has a check mark to remove it from the Quick Access Toolbar.

4. Use the Choose Commands From list to select the command category you want to use.

5. Select the command you want to add.

6. Select Add. The Office RT application adds the command to the custom group or tab.

7. Select a command and then select Move Up or Move Down to position the command within the Quick Access Toolbar. Repeat steps 4 to 7 as needed.

8. Select OK. The Office RT application adds the commands to the Quick Access Toolbar.

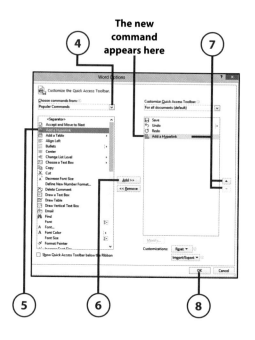

Setting the Office Background

You can add a bit of visual interest to your Office RT applications by applying a background pattern that appears in the title bar.

1. Select File.

2. Select the Account tab.

3. Use the Office Background list to select the pattern you want to use. Office RT applies the pattern to all the Office RT applications.

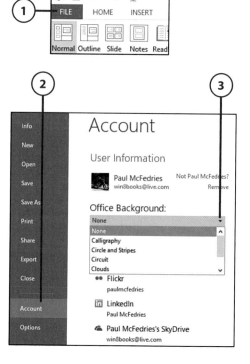

Work with comments

Share an Excel workbook

Track document changes

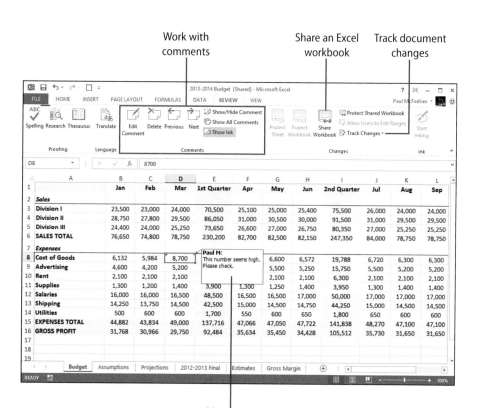

Add comments to a document

Collaborating with Others

Whether you're a company employee, a consultant, or a freelancer, you almost certainly work with other people in one capacity or another. Most of the time, our work with others is informal and consists of ideas exchanged during meetings, phone calls, or email messages. However, we're often called upon to work with others more closely by collaborating with them on a document. This could involve commenting on another person's work, editing someone else's document, or dividing a project among multiple authors. For all of these situations, Office RT offers a number of powerful collaborative tools. This chapter shows you how to use and get the most out of these tools.

Collaborating in Word with Comments and Changes

Microsoft Word is the collaboration champion in the Office suite because, more than any other Office program, Word boasts an impressive collection of tools that enables you to work with other people on a document. In the next few sections, you'll learn about the simplest and most common collaboration tools: comments and tracking changes.

Inserting Comments in a Word Document

If someone asks for your feedback on a document, you could write that feedback in a separate document or in an email message. However, feedback is most useful when it appears in the proper context. That is, if you have a suggestion or critique of a particular word, sentence, or paragraph, the reader will understand that feedback more readily if it appears near the text in question. To do that in Word, you insert a *comment*, a separate section of text that is associated with some part of the original document.

1. Select the text you want to comment on. If you want to comment on a particular word, you can position the cursor within or immediately to the left or right of the word.

2. Select the Review tab.

3. Select New Comment. Word highlights the selected text to indicate that it has an associated comment.

4. Type the comment.

5. Select Close.

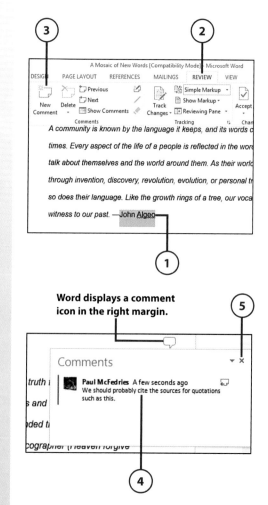

Word displays a comment icon in the right margin.

Editing a Comment

You can edit a comment either by adding to or changing the existing comment text, or by responding to a comment made by another person.

1. Select the icon of the comment you want to edit. The Comments box appears.

2. Edit the comment text as needed.

3. If you want to respond to the comment, select this icon.

4. Type your response.

5. Select Close.

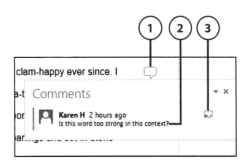

Deleting a Comment

When you no longer need a comment, you can delete it to reduce clutter in the Word document.

1. Select the comment you want to delete.

2. Select the Review tab.

3. Select the top half of the Delete button. Word deletes the comment.

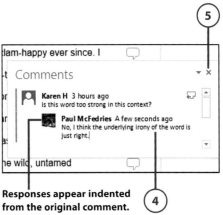

Responses appear indented from the original comment.

Deleting All Comments

If you want a fresh start with a Word document, you can delete all the comments. To do this quickly, select the Review tab, select the bottom half of the Delete button in the Comments group, and then select Delete All Comments in Document.

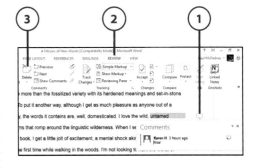

Tracking Changes in a Word Document

A higher level of collaboration occurs when you ask another person to make changes to a document. That is, rather than suggesting changes by using comments, the other person performs the actual changes herself with Word keeping track of all the changes made to the document. This means that any time you or another person makes changes to the original text—including adding, editing, deleting, and formatting the text—Word keeps track of the changes and shows not only what changes were made, but who made them and when.

1. Select the Review tab.

2. Select the top half of the Track Changes button.

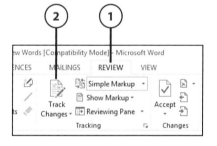

Keyboard Shortcut

You can toggle Track Changes on and off quickly by pressing Ctrl+Shift+E.

Controlling the Display of Comments and Changes

Depending on the document and the number of reviewers, the comments and changes can make a document appear to be quite a mess. Fortunately, Word allows you to filter out particular types of changes, and even changes made by particular reviewers.

These filters are part of Word's Show Markup list, which contains the following six commands that toggle the respective markup on and off:

- **Comments**

- **Ink**

- **Insertions and Deletions**

- **Formatting**

- **Balloons**—This command displays a list that enables you to select which revisions appear in balloons when the reviewing pane is activated. By default, Word only shows comments and formatting changes in balloons, but you can also choose to show all revisions in balloons or all revisions inline (that is, within the text itself).

- **Specific People**—This command displays a list of reviewers so you can toggle the display of changes made by a particular reviewer.

Defining Markup

Markup refers to the icons, font changes, and balloons that indicate the comments and changes reviewers have made to a document.

Word also offers several options for controlling the entire markup in a document. The Display for Review list contains the following four commands:

- **Simple Markup**—This view shows the final version of the document (the version of the document if you accept all the current changes) with the markup only indicated with comment icons in the right margin and revision marks in the left margin.

- **All Markup**—This view shows the final version of the document (the version of the document if you accept all the current changes) with deletions marked as strikethrough, and comments, additions, and formatting changes shown in balloons.

- **No Markup**—This view shows the final version of the document with none of the markup showing (that is, how the document would look if all the changes had been accepted).

- **Original**—This is the original version of the document, before any changes were made (or, more precisely, either before Track Changes was turned on or since the last time all the changes were accepted).

Controlling the Markup Display

By default, Word shows all revisions from all reviewers using the Simple Markup display, but you can change these defaults to ones that you prefer.

1. Select the Review tab.

2. Select Show Markup.

3. Select which types of markup you want to view.

4. Pull down the Display for Review list.

5. Select how you want Word to display the document's markup.

With Simple Markup, all other revisions are indicated with vertical bars in the left margin.

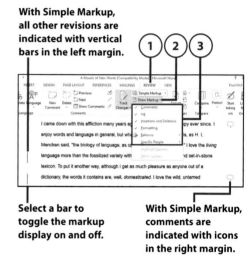

Select a bar to toggle the markup display on and off.

With Simple Markup, comments are indicated with icons in the right margin.

Navigating Comments and Changes

To make sure that you review every comment or change in a document, or to accept or reject comments and changes individually (see the next section), you need to use Word's reviewing navigation tools.

1. Select the Review tab.

2. In the Comments group, select Next to view the next comment in the document.

3. Select Previous to view the previous comment in the document.

Select Show Comments to see all comments instead of just their icons.

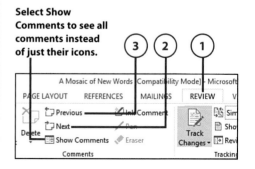

4. In the Changes group, select Next to view the next revision in the document.

5. Select Previous to view the previous revision in the document.

Select Reviewing Pane to see all revisions instead of just their icons.

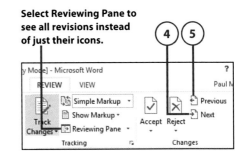

Accepting or Rejecting Comments and Changes

The point of marking up a document is to later on review the changes and then either incorporate some or all of them into the final version or remove those that are not useful or suitable. Word gives you several tools to either accept markup (this action applies to changes only) or reject markup (this action applies to both comments and changes).

1. Select the Review tab.

2. Navigate to the change you want to work with.

3. If you want to accept the change, select the top half of the Accept button.

4. If you want to reject the change, instead, select the top half of the Reject button.

5. Repeat steps 2 to 4 until you've gone through all the changes you want to review.

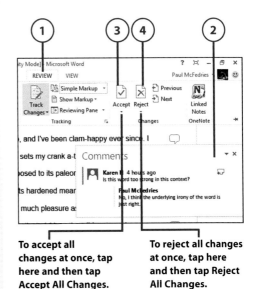

To accept all changes at once, tap here and then tap Accept All Changes.

To reject all changes at once, tap here and then tap Reject All Changes.

ACCEPTING SHOWN CHANGES

In many situations, you want to accept all changes of a certain type (such as formatting or insertions and deletions) and review the rest. To accept all changes of a certain type, first use the Show Markup list to turn off the display of all revisions except the type you want to accept (see "Controlling the Markup Display," earlier in this chapter). Then, in the Review tab, select the bottom half of the Accept button and select Accept All Changes Shown.

You can also accept only the changes made by a particular reviewer. To display the markup for a single reviewer, pull down the Show Markup list, select Specific People, and then select All Reviewers to turn off all markup. Select Show Markup, Specific People again, and this time select the reviewer whose markup you want to accept. Then, in the Review tab, select the bottom half of the Accept button and select Accept All Changes Shown.

Collaborating in Excel with Comments and Changes

As with Word, Excel enables you to collaborate with other people by adding comments and tracking changes. Although these features are implemented slightly differently in Excel, the underlying concepts are basically the same, as you'll see in the next few sections. Later you'll see that Excel also enables you to collaborate by sharing a workbook among multiple users.

Inserting Comments in Cells

The simplest level of collaboration with an Excel workbook is the comment that does not change any worksheet data, but offers notes, suggestions, and critiques of the worksheet content. In Excel, you associate comments with individual cells, not with ranges.

1. Select the cell in which you want to insert the comment.

2. Select the Review tab.

3. Select New Comment. Excel displays an empty comment balloon.

Turning Off the Comment Indicators

If you don't want to see the comment indicators, you can turn them off by choosing File, Options, and then clicking the Advanced tab. In the Display section, select the No Comments or Indicators option and then click OK.

4. Type the comment text.

5. When you are done, tap outside the comment balloon.

Editing a Comment

If you need to make changes to a comment, select the cell, select the Review tab, and then select Edit Comment. Excel opens the comment for editing. Make your changes and then tap outside the comment box. If you need to delete a comment, tap the cell, tap Review, and then tap Delete.

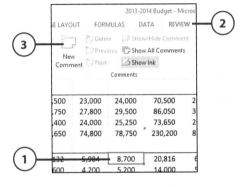

Excel indicates the inserted comment by adding a small red triangle to the upper-right corner of the cell.

Viewing Workbook Comments

By default, Excel indicates commented cells by placing a small, red triangle in the upper-right corner of the cell, but it doesn't display the comment itself. So to read a cell's comment, you must display it by hand.

1. Select the cell that contains the comment you want to view.

2. Select the Review tab.

3. Select Show/Hide Comment. Excel displays the comment.

Viewing with a Mouse

If you have a mouse or trackpad, you can view the comment by hovering the mouse pointer over the cell.

4. To hide the comment, select Show/Hide Comment.

5. Select Next to view the next comment in the worksheet.

6. Select Previous to view the previous comment in the worksheet.

If there are multiple comments, you can display them all by selecting Show All Comments.

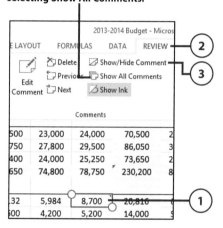

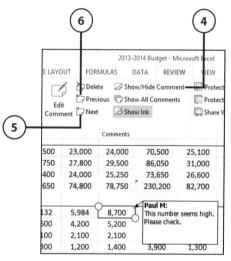

>>>Go Further

DISPLAYING COMMENTS FULL-TIME

If you find yourself constantly displaying comments in a workbook, you can configure Excel to always show them, which saves you from having to display the comments manually. Select File, Options to open the Excel Options dialog box and then select the Advanced tab. In the Display section, select the Comments and Indicators option, and then select OK.

Tracking Worksheet Changes

If you want other people to make changes to a workbook, keeping track of those changes is a good idea so you can either accept or reject them. Like Word, Excel has a Track Changes feature that enables you to do this. When you turn on Track Changes, Excel monitors the activity of each reviewer and stores their cell edits, row and column additions and deletions, range moves, worksheet insertions, and worksheet renames. You can also filter the changes by date, reviewer, or worksheet location.

1. Select the Review tab.

2. Select Track Changes.

3. Select Highlight Changes. Excel displays the Highlight Changes dialog box.

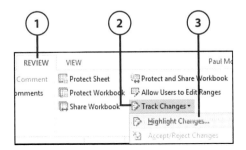

4. Select the Track Changes While Editing check box. (The check box text mentions that "This also shares the workbook." You find out more details on sharing an Excel workbook later in this chapter in the "Sharing an Excel Workbook with Other Users" section.)

5. To filter the displayed changes by time, select the When check box and then use the list to select a time frame.

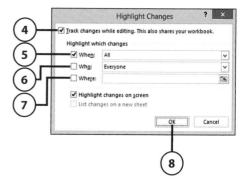

Filtering Changes by Date

To show only the changes that have occurred since a specific date, drop down the When list, select the Since Date item, and then edit the date that Excel displays (the default is the current date).

6. To filter the displayed changes by reviewer, select the Who check box and then select a reviewer or group in the list. At first, this list contains Everyone and Everyone but Me. Later, when other users have made changes, the list will include the name of each reviewer.

7. To filter the displayed changes by range, select the Where check box and then select the range in which you want changes displayed.

8. Select OK. Excel displays a dialog box letting you know that it will save your workbook.

9. Select OK.

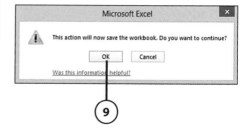

CHANGING HOW LONG EXCEL KEEPS TRACKED CHANGES

By default, Excel keeps track of changes made for the past 30 days. To change the number of days of change history that Excel tracks, select the Review tab and then select Share Workbook to open the Share Workbook dialog box. Select the Advanced tab and then modify the value in the Keep Change History for *X* Days spin box. Select OK to put the new value into effect.

It's Not All Good

UNDERSTANDING TRACK CHANGES LIMITATIONS

When you activate Track Changes, Excel does not track formatting changes. Also, Excel does not allow a number of operations, including the insertion and deletion of ranges and the deletion of worksheets. You can find a complete list of disallowed operations later in this chapter.

Accepting or Rejecting Workbook Changes

The idea behind tracking workbook changes is so that you can review the changes and then either incorporate some or all of them into the final version of the file or remove those that are not useful or suitable.

1. Select the Review tab.
2. Select Track Changes.
3. Select Accept/Reject Changes. If your workbook has unsaved changes, Excel tells you it will save the workbook.

When changes are made to a cell, Excel displays a blue triangle in the upper-left corner of the cell.

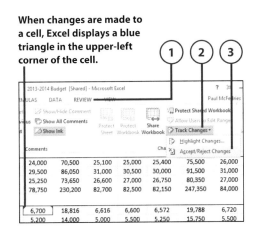

4. Select OK. Excel displays the Select Changes to Accept or Reject dialog box.

5. Use the When, Who, and Where controls to filter the changes, as needed (see the previous section for the details).

6. Select OK. Excel displays the Accept or Reject Changes dialog box and displays a change.

7. Click Accept or Reject. Excel moves to the next change. Repeat this step until you have reviewed all the changes.

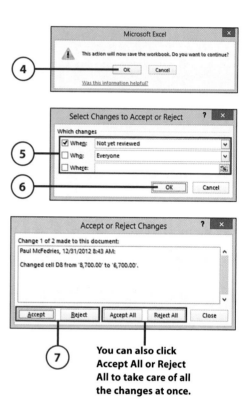

You can also click Accept All or Reject All to take care of all the changes at once.

Sharing an Excel Workbook with Other Users

Most Excel worksheet models are built to analyze data, but that analysis is only as good as the data is accurate. If you are building a model that brings in data from different departments or divisions, you can create a single workbook that you share with other users. This method enables those users to make changes to the workbook, and you can track those changes as described in the previous section. This is why Excel turns on workbook sharing automatically when you activate the Track Changes

feature. Note, however, that the
opposite is not the case. That is, you
can share a workbook without also
tracking changes.

1. Select the Review tab.

2. Select Share Workbook. Excel
   displays the Share Workbook
   dialog box.

3. Select the Allow Changes by More
   Than One User at the Same Time
   check box.

4. Select OK. Excel tells you it will
   save the workbook.

5. Select OK. Excel shares the workbook and displays [Shared] in the
   title bar to remind you that the
   workbook is shared.

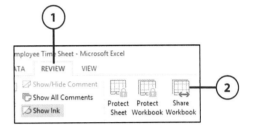

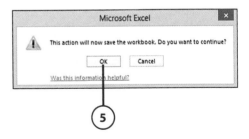

UPDATING A SHARED WORKBOOK ON A SCHEDULE

By default, Excel updates a shared workbook when you save the file. However, you can also configure the workbook to update its changes automatically after a specified number of minutes. Select the Review tab and then select Share Workbook to display the Share Workbook dialog box. Select the Advanced tab. In the Update changes group, select the Automatically Every X Minutes option to have Excel update the workbook using the interval you specify in the spin box (the minimum is 5 minutes; the maximum is 1,440 minutes). You can also elect to have Excel save your changes at the same time or just see the changes made by other users. Select OK to put the new settings into effect.

It's Not All Good

SHARED WORKBOOK RESTRICTIONS

Note that Excel doesn't allow the following operations while a workbook is shared:

- Inserting and deleting ranges (although you can insert and delete entire rows and columns)

- Inserting charts, symbols, pictures, diagrams, objects, and hyperlinks

- Creating or modifying tables or PivotTables

- Importing external data

- Deleting or moving worksheets

- Applying conditional formatting

- Working with scenarios

- Subtotaling, validating, grouping, and outlining data

- Merging cells

- Checking for formula errors

Displaying and Removing Reviewers

While your workbook is shared, you might also want to keep track of who is currently using it.

1. Select the Review tab.

2. Select Share Workbook. Excel displays the Share Workbook dialog box.

3. Select the Editing tab. The Who Has This Workbook Open Now list displays the current reviewers.

4. Select OK.

Excel displays [Shared] in the title bar of a shared workbook.

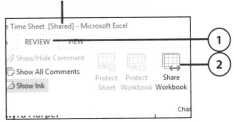

The workbook's current reviewers appear here.

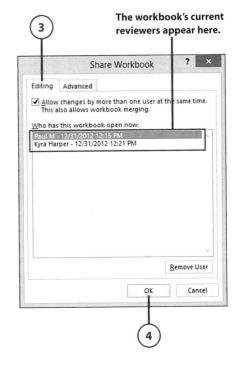

REMOVING A USER

Note that you can prevent a reviewer from using the workbook by clicking the user and then clicking Remove User. You should forcefully remove a user only as a last resort because doing so could easily cause the user to lose unsaved changes. Asking the person directly to save his or her changes and close the workbook is safer (and friendlier).

Handling Sharing Conflicts

If a downside exists to sharing a workbook with other users, it's that occasionally two people will make changes to the same cell. For example, it could happen that another user changes a cell, saves his or her changes, and then you change the same cell before updating. This situation creates a conflict in the workbook versions that must be resolved.

1. Select Save. Before saving, Excel updates the workbook with the changes made by other users. If it detects a conflict, it displays the Resolve Conflicts dialog box.

2. Select which change you want to accept. Excel displays the next conflict. Repeat this step until all the conflicts have been resolved.

3. Select OK.

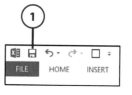

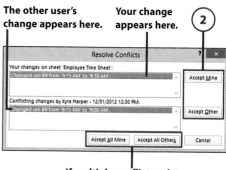

The other user's change appears here.   Your change appears here.

If multiple conflicts exist, you can click one of these buttons to accept all of your or the other user's changes.

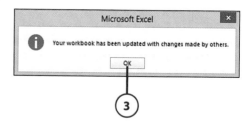

Collaborating with SkyDrive

Collaborating on a document often means storing that document in a location that's accessible by each collaborator. In an office environment, that usually means uploading the document to a shared network folder. What happens if one or more of your collaborators don't have access to your network? You could email the document, but then you end up with multiple copies floating around. A better solution is to place a copy of the document in a SkyDrive folder and then give your collaborators permission to access that folder and edit the document. The rest of this chapter shows you how to do this.

Adding a Document to Your SkyDrive

The first step in collaborating on a document using SkyDrive is to upload the document to your SkyDrive folder.

1. Open the document you want to collaborate on.

2. Select File.

3. Select Save As.

4. Select your SkyDrive location.

5. Select Browse. The Office RT application connects to your SkyDrive and displays it in the Save As dialog box.

6. Select a SkyDrive folder.

7. Adjust the file name, if needed.

8. Select Save. The Office RT application uploads a copy of the document to the SkyDrive folder and opens that copy.

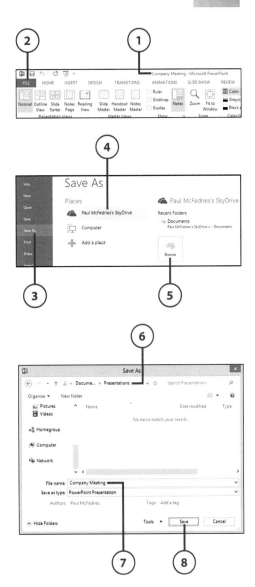

It's Not All Good

WORKING WITH THE SKYDRIVE VERSION

It's important to remember that after you run the Save As command, the Office RT application opens the SkyDrive version of the document on your computer. This means that any changes you make to the document will be reflected in the SkyDrive version of the file, *not* the local version of the file.

Sharing a SkyDrive Folder

With the document you want to collaborate on now uploaded to a folder on your SkyDrive, the next step is to share that folder with other people.

1. Use a web browser to navigate https://skydrive.live.com. If you're not already signed in, the SkyDrive sign-in page appears.

2. Type your Microsoft account email address.

3. Type your Microsoft account password.

4. Select Sign In.

5. Open the SkyDrive folder you want to share.

6. Select Share Folder.

7. Type the email address of the person with whom you want to share the folder. To enter multiple addresses, press Enter after each one.

8. Type a message to your collaborators.

9. To allow other users to edit the documents in the folder, be sure to select the Recipients Can Edit check box.

10. Select Share. SkyDrive sends the sharing email to the recipients.

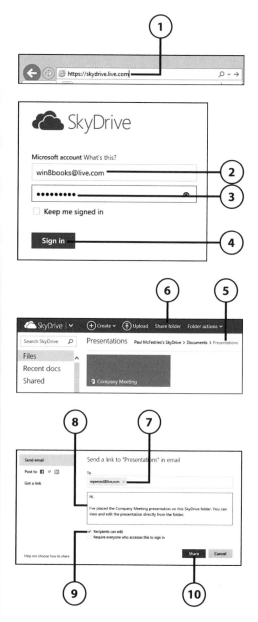

SHARING AN ADDRESS

>>>Go Further

Rather than sending an email to your collaborators, you can get SkyDrive to generate an address for sharing the folder. You could then use that address in a text message, a web page link, or anywhere else that your collaborators can access it. To share an address, select Get a Link. You can then choose from one of three address types. Select View Only to generate an address that allows users to only view the files in the SkyDrive folder, select View and Edit to generate an address that allows users to both view and edit the files in the SkyDrive folder, or select Make Public to generate an address that anyone can use to view the files in the SkyDrive folder.

Index

My Office 2013 RT

Paul McFedries

Your purchase of **My Office 2013 RT** includes access to a free online edition for 45 days through the **Safari Books Online** subscription service. Nearly every Que book is available online through **Safari Books Online**, along with thousands of books and videos from publishers such as Addison-Wesley Professional, Cisco Press, Exam Cram, IBM Press, O'Reilly Media, Prentice Hall, Sams, and VMware Press.

Safari Books Online is a digital library providing searchable, on-demand access to thousands of technology, digital media, and professional development books and videos from leading publishers. With one monthly or yearly subscription price, you get unlimited access to learning tools and information on topics including mobile app and software development, tips and tricks on using your favorite gadgets, networking, project management, graphic design, and much more.

Activate your FREE Online Edition at informit.com/safarifree

STEP 1:   Enter the coupon code: AKCHFAA.

STEP 2:   New Safari users, complete the brief registration form.
Safari subscribers, just log in.

If you have difficulty registering on Safari or accessing the online edition,
please e-mail customer-service@safaribooksonline.com